COWS on the MOOVE

COWS on the MOOVE

48
Tales from
a Paradelle Universe

volume one

as told by
Old Man Crowe

authorHOUSE®

AuthorHouse™ LLC
1663 Liberty Drive
Bloomington, IN 47403
www.authorhouse.com
Phone: 1-800-839-8640

Published by AuthorHouse   08/27/2013

ISBN: 978-1-4817-5827-7 (sc)
ISBN: 978-1-4918-3240-0 (e)

Any people depicted in stock imagery provided by Thinkstock are models, and such images are being used for illustrative purposes only.
Certain stock imagery © Thinkstock.

This book is printed on acid-free paper.

Because of the dynamic nature of the Internet, any web addresses or links contained in this book may have changed since publication and may no longer be valid. The views expressed in this work are solely those of the author and do not necessarily reflect the views of the publisher, and the publisher hereby disclaims any responsibility for them.

Chronology of Paradelles ... Volume One nos. 1 to 48

An Introduction to a Paradelle Universe ... 2009

In January 2006 I discovered the Paradelle form in a book of poems by Billy Collins. It was like watching a parallel world open up in front of me. In the uncompromising structure of the form I saw my possibilities for creative expression expand out into unbounded potentiality. A Paradelle Universe summoned me and I eagerly leaped; why deny the call of destiny? A few days later, the forces of intention, inspiration and conspiratorial external events converged and I was on my way ... I walked into a bathroom that smelled like a wet dog. The impact turned poetic, and *A Paradelle for a Wet Dog* was born.

It was the combination of this initial success, and the seductive call to see what else was possible, that absorbed me into this practice. No other form of writing has asked as much of me, and given as much of itself, as the Paradelle form. It has become a spiritual practice in its own right, requiring and developing, the qualities of surrender, faith and trust. One never knows how the poem will turn out; or what obstacles one will encounter in the process. As a vehicle for their transmission, I can only trust the process and focus on the work thats before me. Miracles occur when we can participate with our faith.

What is a Paradelle? Its a new poetic form consisting of 4 verses, with each verse containing 6 lines. In the first 3 verses, the 1st and 2nd lines repeat and match exactly, as do the 3rd and 4th. In the 5th and 6th lines, the words of the 1st and 3rd are reorganized and re-expressed. All the words must be used and no other words can be added. In the 4th verse, only the words of the 3 previous verses can be used to create each of the 6 lines. In total there are 24 lines, 12 are static and fixed, until they're copied, disassembled and re-worded into the other 12. In short, its a very constructive process, and it requires a fair amount of focus, patience, and commitment. Not to mention; allowing the words to have their own voice.

The creative potential of the Paradelle structure is found in the multiple levels of interrelationships in and between: words, meaning, and imagery. And in the evolving coherency of the change in positions and perspectives that can be expressed by using the same words to create each line out of the other. Even to the level of sculpturing the sentences themselves and their line position in relationship to the words in other lines. The 4th verse in particular, offers the possibility to create poetry as a visual art form in and of itself. The Paradelle is subliminal as well as surreal and rhetorical, subtle and veiled, as well as direct; and advocating or questioning a particular point of view. This paragraph is but an example in free form.

A Paradelle is a poem that speaks to you. You allow it to speak to you by listening to it as you recite it. How do you recite a Paradelle? You recite a paradelle by letting it speak to you. And in this speaking, it offers **you** the opportunity to speak as you have never spoken before. A paradelle is a poem to both be engaged by and to engage in. And just as the words have their own voice, you need to have your own voice in reading them. A Paradelle is not a passive poem, so it can't be read in a passive voice, it needs to be read expressively, demonstratively, in an authoritative and engaging voice.

Poetry has the potential to revitalize language, and to re-energize the consciousness of those who speak and read it.

Pretend that you are hosting a news show, and that each Paradelle is a news report coming in from somewhere out in the Paradelle Universe. Stand in front of a mirror with an open mind, and play with imitating the voice of a politician or a news anchor, actor, Radio DJ, TV preacher, salesman, your boss, a cultural icon or an affected accent. A Paradelle is Stand Up Poetry, it was created as a joke, its a form of oratory entertainment; the prosaic privilege of a poor Kings Fool.

Or get together with some friends; add your chosen libations, and get down and loose with it. Take turns being the fool, reminding the King of the conditions in his Kingdom ... of the intrigues and corruptions of his royal court. And of course, just being the royal fool yourself and having fun; stepping off the edge of a cliff while testing the limits of poetic license.

Speak as if you were on stage and in a play. Let the words express themselves, and suggest to you the circumstances and the action of each Paradelle. What kind of play would it be? What is happening in the play? Who are you, and what would your role be? Are you speaking of something, or for, or about something? The Paradelle is a soliloquy ... the actor, while speaking to himself; steps outside of the play to speak before the audience. Be expressive with your arms and voice and add your own need or appetite for drama or comedy to your delivery. Think of it as karaoke poetry or a cappella rap.

A Paradelle is participatory poetry telling a story. A story that can be put on and worn as a character. Is there a character in you that could come forward and give voice to a particular paradelle? To say things you've wanted to say, but never had the context or form? Things you've wanted to say, but lacked the expressive means which allowed you to move or release old, stagnant energy and emotion? Maybe things you never even knew were in you until reading a particular paradelle.

Playing with the Paradelles in this way encourages and supports a new sense of personal empowerment by giving voice to the outrageous, the absurd, the nonsensical and the true. But to say to who? To whom would you want to speak in such an outlandish and unapologetically direct way? The possibility is yours to discover. And while words have their meaning; its the energy that can be expressed through the words thats important. Allowing oneself to be impacted by what has been said, and how its been said, brings these energies and emotions to our awareness, where they can be explored.

Reading from *Tales from a Paradelle Universe*, is an investment in ones self, not in me as their author. These poems are not about me as much as they are about the situations and circumstances we all experience as human beings living in the modern world. They express a universal experience of life more than my own individual experience. True they are colored by my own perceptions, but that perspective is of a character ... not my identity. In this way, the poem is open for someone else to bring their own identity to bear on the character of each Paradelle; and give their own flavor and flair to the poem.

Put a Paradelle in your mouth and feel what shape the words take as they're spoken. Take the ones that speak to you and make them your own. Paradelles are high milage poetry, to be read again and again. So get down with yourself and enjoy the ride. The Paradelle Universe is an accessible and intelligent alternative reality. Participating is as easy as speaking.

An Invitation to Participate ... 2013

In its own distinct way, the Paradelle is an expression of an ever evolving narrative potentiality; one that can always be revisited and rewritten. In much the same way; as our personal narratives can change and evolve over time in becoming more and more coherent; the changing nature of the 5th and 6th lines and the entire 4th verse allows for reinterpretation.

A Paradelle makes a provocative statement; that is symphonically varied and reorganized; redeveloped and transformed. Its structure is a form of phrase modulated poetry; evocative images that can be read obliquely; horizontally and vertically. The form is an opportunity to renew our relationship to language and life by redefining the context and our usage of words

If reading a paradelle elicits a response or reaction in you by what is being said ... one motivating enough to pick up a pen and participate in the conversation ... I have provided a blank surface on the back of each Paradelle for you to write down the very same words that I've played with, and discover what they can say for you; or perhaps to let speak for themselves.

I invite you to journey along with me as I explore, in the telling of each tale; the alternative realities of a Paradelle Universe

A Paradelle for a Wet Dog

Why does your breath smell like a wet dog?
Why does your breath smell like a wet dog?
What has your tongue been rolling in?
What has your tongue been rolling in?
Why does your dog, smell like what a wet
tongue ... has been rolling your breath in?

Profusely panting, the harried rabbit finally escapes.
Profusely panting, the harried rabbit finally escapes.
A lost dog howls in a thicket of confusion.
A lost dog howls in a thicket of confusion.
Profusely lost in a dog thicket; the rabbit finally
escapes a panting confusion of harried howls.

With a friend like a dog, who needs a policeman?
With a friend like a dog, who needs a policeman?
Crossing the street in the pouring rain?
Crossing the street in the pouring rain?
Crossing the street with a friend in the pouring rain,
who needs a dog like a policeman?

Pouring in a dog ...
like a wet rabbit lost in a thicket of rain ...
a profusely harried tongue howls like a panting policeman.
Who needs the confusion your dog has been rolling in?
Why? Crossing a street with a friend does what?
Finally; the dog smell escapes your breath.

A Paradelle for Two Tails/Tales

Every dog has two tails,
Every dog has two tails,
one to wag and one to tell.
one to wag and one to tell.
And tails wag to everyone;
to tell one dog has two.

Happy dogs tell tales to please the moon.
Happy dogs tell tales to please the moon.
Howling at the sight of the cats' pajamas.
Howling at the sight of the cats' pajamas.
Happy at the sight of the howling moon,
dogs tell tales to please the cats' pajamas.

Frightened dogs hang their tails in silence,
Frightened dogs hang their tails in silence,
mumbling ancestral prayers beneath their bark.
mumbling ancestral prayers beneath their bark.
Their tails mumbling in ancestral prayers,
dogs hang their bark beneath frightened silence.

Ancestral dogs bark beneath the moon.
Frightened cats' hang their pajamas in the silence;
mumbling at the sight of one happy dog.
Howling, dogs wag tails to please their prayers,
and to tell tales to everyone;
two tails has to tell.

A Paradelle for a Ride in a Fast Car

What dog can resist a ride in a fast car,
What dog can resist a ride in a fast car,
with fresh skunk in the air on a summer afternoon?
with fresh skunk in the air on a summer afternoon?
What skunk ... can resist a ride, on a fast dog,
in a summer car, within the fresh afternoon air?

In doggedly nosing her face in the wind;
In doggedly nosing her face in the wind;
how fast the smell flies when you're having a good time.
how fast the smell flies when you're having a good time.
Having a goodly smell nosing her fast in the face,
how the wind flies ... when you're dogged in time.

Never slowing down to bark at the asphalt,
Never slowing down to bark at the asphalt,
the heat of the tires ... growls in agreement.
the heat of the tires ... growls in agreement.
Never slowing down to bark in agreement,
the heat of the asphalt growls at the tires.

When you're nosing in on a good time ...
never slowing down the afternoon
to doggedly growl at a summer skunk ...
what dog can resist a car with fresh air in the tires?
Having a ride in the heat, the asphalt flies in the wind!
How fast the smell of agreement ... barks in her face.

A Paradelle for Falling Down

Seen upwards from the bottom of the fall,
Seen upwards from the bottom of the fall,
the suspense of falling is preserved in the gravity of a look.
the suspense of falling is preserved in the gravity of a look.
Seen upwards ... from the suspense of gravity,
the bottom of the fall is preserved in the falling of a look.

The circumference of the soul is not a circle.
The circumference of the soul is not a circle.
The hand that measures fate opens no portals.
The hand that measures fate opens no portals.
The a ... portal ... no circumference measures ...
is not the soul that circles the open hands of fate.

Entering through the empty eye, I remember what I forgot ...
Entering through the empty eye, I remember what I forgot ...
in the recollection of heavens descending sunlight.
in the recollection of heavens descending sunlight.
Remembering what the recollection of I forgot. Entering
through heavens eye ... I descend in the empty sunlight.

In what I forgot of the fall ...
descending from no recollection of the suspense ...
a hand opens in the upwards measures of gravity.
I remember the look! The heavens falling!! The empty bottom of fate!!!
The eye of sunlight is preserved entering through a portal.
The soul is not seen ... that circles the circumference.

A Paradelle for Dogs

Isn't every dog the image of its master;
Isn't every dog the image of its master;
surrendering to the service of love?
surrendering to the service of love?
Isn't service to the master of its love;
the surrendering image of every dog?

The muddy paw prints won't mar the marble.
The muddy paw prints won't mar the marble,
walking through a temple of worship and awe.
walking through a temple of worship and awe.
The marble paw prints, walking through the awe
of a temple ... won't mar and muddy the worship.

Delivered by the one who can fetch its respect,
Delivered by the one who can fetch its respect,
a dog sees god when it barks for its own dinner.
a dog sees god when it barks for its own dinner.
When its dinner barks for its own dog; can a god
fetch ... the one who sees it delivered by respect?

When a muddy dog who can fetch one of its own;
sees a god walking through the temple ...
and surrendering; the dog barks its respect
for the worship of ... of marble paw prints ...
it won't mar the master to service the image of awe.
Isn't every dinner delivered by its love?

A Paradelle for Every Dog

After long nights of patient waiting,
After long nights of patient waiting,
every dog is born to have its day.
every dog is born to have its day.
Long after waiting to have its dog,
every day is born of patient nights.

The song in every dog will still be heard,
The song in every dog will still be heard,
in the cathedrals of the human heart.
in the cathedrals of the human heart.
Will the song heard In the cathedrals ...
still be of the dog in every human heart?

The presence of the dog is legendary,
The presence of the dog is legendary,
in sanctifying every threshold between our world and their own.
in sanctifying every threshold between our world and their own.
Between their presence, and the threshold of our own ...
every dog is legendary in sanctifying the world.

Between still nights in our cathedrals ...
and long after their world is to have its own,
the song of the dog will be heard waiting ...
in the patient; every day presence of every dog.
In sanctifying the threshold of the human heart ...
every dog is born legendary.

A Paradelle for a Sympathetic Prefix

A portion of each paragraph is written to conceal,
A portion of each paragraph is written to conceal,
the confession of a paranoid passion for ideals.
the confession of a paranoid passion for ideals.
For the passion of paranoid ideals; a paragraph,
is written to conceal each portion of a confession.

The eyes of every parasite are focused to be sure,
The eyes of every parasite are focused to be sure,
to examine every paradox that claims to have the cure.
to examine every paradox that claims to have the cure.
Eyes that have to be focused ... to examine the claims
of every paradox ... are the sure cure to every parasite.

Perched up on a parapet, lonely in the night,
Perched up on a parapet, lonely in the night,
sits the bird of paradise, a parakeets delight.
sits the bird of paradise, a parakeets delight.
Perched upon a para-pet delight, the parakeet
sits in a lonely birds paradise of the night.

Perched upon the written confession of ... of a parasite;
each paragraph a paradox for the sure eyes of night.
The para-pet sits to conceal the paranoid ideals,
that claim to be every parakeet's paradise.
The passions are delighted to have a lonely bird
to examine ... every portion of a cure is in focus.

13

A Paradelle for Suffering an Obstinate Fate

It was one more lousy moment in the endless loop of time,
It was one more lousy moment in the endless loop of time,
the repetitious evidence ... life is inherently unkind.
the repetitious evidence ... life is inherently unkind.
It was the lousy ... repetitious loop of unkind evidence;
life is the inherently endless, one more moment in time.

I went to smell a daffodil; I stopped to smell a rose,
I went to smell a daffodil; I stopped to smell a rose,
but all I found within myself was a buzzing up my nose.
but all I found within myself was a buzzing up my nose.
I found a smell within myself ... a daffodil ... a rose?
I went buzzing up to all, but I was stopped to smell my nose.

So I sat in meditation in an effort just to be,
So I sat in meditation in an effort just to be,
believing that compassion, could release my misery.
believing that compassion, could release my misery.
So ... I sat in meditation ... believing that an effort
to be in misery could release my just compassion.

Believing that compassion ... is a rose I could smell,
I sat to smell an inherently unkind daffodil.
It was a lousy moment to release evidence up my nose.
So, just to be in the meditation, I went in one more time.
In the repetitious effort, I found a loop of life within myself.
My buzzing misery stopped. All was but endless.

A Paradelle for the Broadcast News

There's been a News development in stem cell research.
There's been a News development in stem cell research.
God has filed a lawsuit over copyright violations.
God has filed a lawsuit over copyright violations.
There's a Development! Lawsuit Filed Over Violations!
Stem Cell Copy a Has Been! Right Renews Search in God!

Being himself and no stranger to the law,
Being himself and no stranger to the law,
God will represent his own interests.
God will represent his own interests.
And being no stranger to his own interests ...
the law will represent God himself.

Claiming that insight and innovation belongs to everyone,
Claiming that insight and innovation belongs to everyone,
the Corporations involved have counter sued for damages.
the Corporations involved have counter sued for damages.
And claiming that the counter damages belong to everyone;
Corporations involved have sued insights for innovation.

Claiming development and innovation rights for Himself;
God has been counter sued over His own Incorporation.
Being there's no new insight involved;
and research violations interests everyone ...
God will have to stem the lawsuits filed.
A stranger law belongs to the cell damage that a copy represents.

A Paradelle for the Replaceable Dog

Some people search their minds for the replaceable dog,
Some people search their minds for the replaceable dog,
reconstructing their memories of long walks and friendship.
reconstructing their memories of long walks and friendship.
Some minds search their memories for replaceable people,
reconstructing long walks, and the friendship of their dog.

Some search their hearts for the passage of time,
Some search their hearts for the passage of time,
waiting for a possible tomorrow and the fresh bark of a new day.
waiting for a possible tomorrow and the fresh bark of a new day.
Some hearts wait for a new bark ... searching the possible
for a time of passage ... and the fresh day of their tomorrow.

Myself, I search within the soul of the dog who has gone beyond,
Myself, I search within the soul of the dog who has gone beyond,
to fetch the wind and take his place, unique among the stars.
to fetch the wind and take his place, unique among the stars.
I take the search of the wind within, who has gone to fetch the dog,
and place among the stars myself, his unique soul ... beyond!

I take the dog for long walks and search beyond the passage of the day;
... for his friendship ... and possible place among my memories.
Some people, search to fetch the time gone of their minds;
reconstructing their hearts within the replaceable stars of tomorrow.
Some search their soul, for the waiting bark of the wind ...
and a unique dog; who has a fresh ... new self.

A Paradelle For Kind of Like

If I was kind of like, movement without pause,
If I was kind of like, movement without pause,
would I be nearer to my goal of standing still?
would I be nearer to my goal of standing still?
Standing still without movement, would kind
of be like, I was nearer to my goal of, if I pause.

If I could be like, whatever I wanted to be?
If I could be like, whatever I wanted to be?
Would I lose anything by remaining who I am?
Would I lose anything by remaining who I am?
If I could be like, whatever who I wanted to be;
would anything remain I, by losing I am?

If I was kind of like, full of shadows like the sun,
If I was kind of like, full of shadows like the sun,
could I pass before the day and not be seen by anyone?
could I pass before the day and not be seen by anyone?
If the day was like, not seen by the sun, could I like,
pass before any kind of shadows; and be full of one I?

Before I pass by any nearer to the shadows of standing still,
could I not pause; and ... kind of like,
lose any remaining movement I wanted to be?
Like if I ... whatever kind of would be thing was my goal;
if I ... I could be seen by the full sun of who I am;
would be like ... like ... one day without if I was.

A Paradelle for the Great Smoker

The old smoker said the pigs here are great,
The old smoker said the pigs here are great,
and my smoked ham is the best in the world.
and my smoked ham is the best in the world.
The ham here is great ... said the old smoker,
and my pigs are the best smoked the in world.

Rolling pigs in a blanket, with the best cabbage on the lake,
Rolling pigs in a blanket, with the best cabbage on the lake,
the smoker lights up the world with an oink and a wink.
the smoker lights up the world with an oink and a wink.
And with the lake world rolling the smokers on a blanket;
the cabbage lights up an oink with the best wink in a pig.

After lunch, a ham in hand, and heading for the boat,
After lunch, a ham in hand, and heading for the boat,
the stoned pathway leads down to the wooden dock.
the stoned pathway leads down to the wooden dock.
And after heading for the stoned ham, the dockhand
leads down the pathway, to lunch in a wooden boat.

Rolling pigs in a ... a boat blanket; an old smoker said:
"my stoned ham and cabbage is the best on the lake."
Here ... with the world heading for the great ham ...
the pigs are down the path and in with the smoker!
After lunch, the dockhand lights up a smoked oink;
and leads the way to the best wooden wink in the world.

A Paradelle for Not Quite Yet

Grandfather Nothing had an extraordinary idea,
Grandfather Nothing had an extraordinary idea,
create a vacuum and go with the flow.
create a vacuum and go with the flow.
A grand nothing had vacuum father the idea:
create with an extraordinary flow and go.

It was possibly the most ordinary day of his life.
It was possibly the most ordinary day of his life.
Something was sure to come out of it.
Something was sure to come out of it.
It was possibly his most ordinary someday.
The sure thing of it, was to come out of llfe.

Anytime nothingness encounters a possibility,
Anytime nothingness encounters a possibility,
nothing will ever be the same.
nothing will ever be the same.
Nothingness will ever be a possibility;
anytime nothing encounters the same.

It was possibly the most ordinary possibility;
create an extraordinary life out of nothing.
Anytime Father Flow encounters a vacuum of will ...
the same day nothing ... and a grand idea,
his nothingness was sure to go ...
with the ever something it had become.

A Paradelle for Arcata

Luxury in the heart of ignorance; a brand new begging bowl sanctifies a sidewalk shrine,
Luxury in the heart of ignorance; a brand new begging bowl sanctifies a sidewalk shrine,
as dirty hippies with dogs wait to be blessed; nibbling on the generosity of strangers.
as dirty hippies with dogs wait to be blessed; nibbling on the generosity of strangers.
As a heart shrine sanctifies the hippies, begging to be with a brand new bowl of luxury,
sidewalk strangers wait in dirty ignorance ... nibbling on the blessed generosity of dogs.

Smoking cigarettes, scanning the street with the damaged look of a drunken hunger,
Smoking cigarettes, scanning the street with the damaged look of a drunken hunger,
or to be indifferent to whatever the weather and barking up a storm? No dog wants that!
or to be indifferent to whatever the weather and barking up a storm? No dog wants that!
With a storm of cigarettes smoking up the drunken street ... no dog wants the weather
to be scanning what ever and barking a look that damaged or indifferent to the hunger.

Meanwhile, the fog rolls in and out again with the timeless toiling of the tide;
Meanwhile, the fog rolls in and out again with the timeless toiling of the tide;
as waves of the unwashed, wash up not washed, wherever the tide will take them.
as waves of the unwashed, wash up not washed, wherever the tide will take them.
And meanwhile: toiling in the washed again tide; as the wash will not take them
with the unwashed waves of wherever ... the timeless tide rolls up out of the fog.

As a dog rolls in the blessed out cigarettes ... barking with the tide and begging
to be the storm ... washed up hippies, smoking a brand new bowl with the timeless look
of drunken luxury, weather the fog of unwashed ignorance. Scanning the mean sidewalk,
damaged strangers nibbling on dirty whatever; wash again as waves, wherever the dogs
up the street; or the tide of hunger will take them. And while no heart wants to be
that indifferent ... not to a toiling of within ... a shrine of generosity sanctifies the wait.

A Paradelle for the Illiteration of Doggerel (Illiteration: the process of becoming illiterate)

When the doggerel of the day degenerates into well-practiced dogma,
When the doggerel of the day degenerates into well-practiced dogma,
reckless poetry hounds run rabid, in a ragged, wild abandonment of content and form.
reckless poetry hounds run rabid, in a ragged, wild abandonment of content and form.
When the abandonment of rabid dogma degenerates into wild content and reckless form,
the hounds of well-practiced doggerel run poetry ragged in a day.

Gnawing on nothingness with the privileged indulgence of a new born rat,
Gnawing on nothingness with the privileged indulgence of a new born rat,
their speech bears the marks of mangled meaning ... comments: clumsy, clawing and cute.
their speech bears the marks of mangled meaning ... comments: clumsy, clawing and cute.
Gnawing on meaning with the clumsy indulgence of new born mangled speech;
their clawing comments and a cute nothingness bear the marks of privileged rats.

In propagating propaganda, illiteration sinks jagged teeth into their visceral experience,
In propagating propaganda, illiteration sinks jagged teeth into their visceral experience,
ignorant tongues tear flesh off living bone; the innocent instrument of rhythm and rhyme.
ignorant tongues tear flesh off living bone; the innocent instrument of rhythm and rhyme.
Propagating inexperience, the ignorant instrument of propaganda; their teeth tear living
illiteration off flesh and bone; visceral rhythm sinks innocent tongues into jagged rhyme.

When doggerel degenerates the wild illiteration and reckless rhythm of rhyme
... and visceral dogma bears the nothingness of a cute new rat ... inexperience
sinks ignorant teeth into the tongues indulgence of propagating mangled speech.
Content with their bone ragged abandonment; their rabid hounds clawing and gnawing
inborn meaning off of the innocent day ... clumsy comments practiced on living flesh
form into a well-run instrument of propaganda. Privileged poetry marks the jagged tear.

A Paradelle for a Beeping Bikini

The hot sun baking on the soft white sand, a woman in a beeping bikini reacts in alarm,
The hot sun baking on the soft white sand, a woman in a beeping bikini reacts in alarm,
recoiling with disgust from the electronic mandate to conform ... retreat into the shade.
recoiling with disgust from the electronic mandate to conform ... retreat into the shade.
Shade; the conman, on retreat from sun baking a form into the sand, reacts in disgust
to a date with the soft recoiling woman in the beeping white-hot electronic bikini alarm.

"The latest in amazing ultra violet beachwear protection for her; is a beeping swimsuit."
"The latest in amazing ultra violet beachwear protection for her; is a beeping swimsuit."
"But, how to tell which tone is your own on a crowded beach ... is anybody's guess."
"But, how to tell which tone is your own on a crowded beach ... is anybody's guess."
"Tell Violet! The beeping latest in amazing protection for her ... is crowded beachwear!"
"But a ... how to guess which swimsuit is your ultra own on anybody's tone; is a beach!"

As the descending sun pauses above the horizon, bathing the shore in radiant light,
As the descending sun pauses above the horizon, bathing the shore in radiant light,
she lingers, beeping and alone, sleeping beneath an umbrella the size of a tour bus.
she lingers, beeping and alone, sleeping beneath an umbrella the size of a tour bus.
Sun bathing alone beneath the horizon, an umbrella lingers in light, as the descending
tour bus, beeping and radiant, the size of ... a ... pauses above the sleeping she shore.

Recoiling on the baking hot sand, Violet is beeping in retreat from the sunbathing beach.
Shade, sleeping in anybody's beachwear, reacts in alarm to a radiant date with the sun.
Ana lingers in disgust on the ultra crowded umbrella bus, alone but for the size of the tour.
A man pauses above the shore to guess which woman is beeping beneath the horizon ...
and to tell her bikini how amazing she is. The latest form in electronic protection?
A swimsuit beeping a soft white light ... as your own condescending tone?

A Paradelle for Arcata Number Two

Dirty dreadlocked voyeurs slumming through the hidden heartache of America,
Dirty dreadlocked voyeurs slumming through the hidden heartache of America,
trust fund hippies beg change for the pleasure of pretense, posing as poverty's children.
trust fund hippies beg change for the pleasure of pretense, posing as poverty's children.
Voyeurs of poverty's heartache, dreadlocked children, posing as hippies beg the trust
of dirty pleasure ... fund the hidden pretense for change slumming through America.

Disappearing into a phony fog, fake deadbeats play among the damaged and deranged,
Disappearing into a phony fog, fake deadbeats play among the damaged and deranged,
falsely forlorn losers occupying the forgotten territory of the legitimately lost.
falsely forlorn losers occupying the forgotten territory of the legitimately lost.
Fog damaged; forgotten deadbeats ... legitimately lost among the phony and the fake.
Disappearing into the deranged territory of losers ... falsely occupying a forlorn play.

Rebelling against the privilege of their parents, the fashionably destitute and stylishly deprived;
Rebelling against the privilege of their parents, the fashionably destitute and stylishly deprived;
defy their self contempt by counting coins ... concealing their jewelry beneath scruffy clothes.
defy their self contempt by counting coins ... concealing their jewelry beneath scruffy clothes.
And concealing their contempt beneath stylishly scruffy clothes, the fashionably self deprived
defy their parents jewelry by rebelling against counting the coins of their destitute privilege.

Stylishly occupying the lost territory of phony America, the fashionably dreadlocked
beg for scruffy clothes, concealing self contempt beneath the pretense of their jewelry.
Slumming through the privilege of destitute pleasure; counting their coins among poverty's
losers. Falsely posing as forlorn children ... their parents play-fund hidden by the damaged
and fake change ... forgotten deadbeats trust deranged voyeurs disappearing into a dirty fog;
and defy hippies rebelling against the heartache of the legitimately deprived.

A Paradelle for Cows on the Moove

Cows on the moove, stop dead in their tracks, considering the meaning of moo la la.
Cows on the moove, stop dead in their tracks, considering the meaning of moo la la.
When encountering questionable livestock, be polite to inquire - how now Dow Cow?
When encountering questionable livestock, be polite to inquire - how now Dow Cow?
When encountering questionable Dow stock, be polite to inquire the meaning of cows
dead in their tracks. Stop considering the moove on moo la la. How? Live cow now!

The Cow Crossing Advisory Group rejected the call to increase monitoring in the fields.
The Cow Crossing Advisory Group rejected the call to increase monitoring in the fields.
So now, each time you take cows out to pasture, be sure to leave their dance back in the barn.
So now, each time you take cows out to pasture, be sure to leave their dance back in the barn.
Advisory: now be sure to increase the call to dance in each take-out cow you so pasture.
In time the rejected cows leave the group, crossing their fields back to monitoring the barn.

Wandering free-range roaming cows, fenceless and alert to any a ... weirdness around them,
Wandering free-range roaming cows, fenceless and alert to any a ... weirdness around them,
see a roadside cow pause to call at a crossing ... obviously the cow doesn't know moo.
see a roadside cow pause to call at a crossing ... obviously the cow doesn't know moo.
A wandering cow doesn't pause at a fenceless crossing. And free to see any weirdness
roaming the range around them; roadside cows obviously know to call a moo cow alert.

Encountering a questionable advisory ... rejected at the crossing ... cows on the moove dance
to see the increase in their stock of moo la moo la. Crossing the barn, cows monitoring the Dow,
call to take back any roadside cow out wandering the range. Alert to free roaming cow weirdness,
polite cows pause to inquire how ... considering the fenceless pasture now around them.
Each time a group doesn't know when to call in, you leave cow tracks in their fields!
Stop meaning to be so obviously dead sure ... be alive and cow now!

A Paradelle for ... If the Buddha's Teaching had Included a Dog

If the Buddha's teaching had included a dog, would they walk the earth in meditation?
If the Buddha's teaching had included a dog, would they walk the earth in meditation?
Breathing together in the present moment, walking, inhaling, exhaling, no self, no other.
Breathing together in the present moment, walking, inhaling, exhaling, no self, no other.
If walking the earth had included inhaling the Buddha's teaching ... exhaling meditation,
breathing together ... would they, in no other moment, walk the no self present in a dog?

With compassion for the suffering of all others, and a sloppy kiss for condolences,
With compassion for the suffering of all others, and a sloppy kiss for condolences,
the embrace of a dogs heart gives unconditioned comfort to everyone in need of love.
the embrace of a dogs heart gives unconditioned comfort to everyone in need of love.
With unconditioned compassion for suffering a sloppy kiss, the comfort of a dog's heart
gives condolences to all others ... and for everyone ... in need of the embrace of love.

Seated in concentrated meditation, forever faithful to the eternal now, free to be love at last,
Seated in concentrated meditation, forever faithful to the eternal now, free to be love at last,
the dog, hearing the call of devotion, lifted up its ears, the moment Buddha began his walk.
the dog, hearing the call of devotion, lifted up its ears, the moment Buddha began his walk.
Forever seated in faithful love; its ears now hearing the concentrated call of his meditation;
the eternal Buddha devotion lifted the dog up to walk. At last began the moment to be free.

The unconditioned love of the dog gives Buddha's concentrated comfort to everyone.
With its ears lifted up and free, they walk the earth together ... breathing all condolences
into a moment in need of forever ... exhaling the eternal self ... inhaling no other moment,
the Buddha began hearing ... of the call to be now ... present in the dog's love for walking.
Teaching others in the compassion of his meditation included a walk for the suffering heart.
Now if a dog had no faithful kiss, would sloppy devotion, at last embrace seated meditation?

A Paradelle for the Puppeteers

The Government Minister of the Office of Other Peoples Money declared today:
The Government Minister of the Office of Other Peoples Money declared today:
that success and failure are of equal value, as long as the powerless and the poor foot the bill.
that success and failure are of equal value, as long as the powerless and the poor foot the bill.
And Bill Long, Office Minister, declared that today, the success of money and the failure
of the people's government are as equal as the value of the other poor powerless foot.

The Director of the Committee to Protect the Budgets of Over-Inflated Agencies says,
The Director of the Committee to Protect the Budgets of Over-Inflated Agencies says,
in order to prosecute the war on error, attention must be given to ignoring the facts.
in order to prosecute the war on error, attention must be given to ignoring the facts.
The Committee says: in order to ... to protect the agencies of over-inflated facts; given
the director's budget to prosecute; attention must be on ignoring the ... the error of war.

The Ambassador of Arms agrees; the business of destruction is good for the economy.
The Ambassador of Arms agrees; the business of destruction is good for the economy.
Pushing prices down in the U.S. and repression up overseas, keeps our balance of trade.
Pushing prices down in the U.S. and repression up overseas, keeps our balance of trade.
Our Ambassador of Overseas Destruction agrees; the business of arms is good for the
U.S. economy; and in the balance of pushing up trade; repression keeps the prices down.

The Ambassador of Failure declared today: 'the Government over inflated the success
of destruction overseas'. The Office of the Committee of Other Peoples Business says:
'that in order to protect the Director of the War on Facts; equal value and money must be
given to the budgets of the agencies ignoring the error.' Bill Foot, the Minister of Repression
agrees, and keeps balance down in the U.S. trade of arms. And as long as the poor
are powerless to prosecute our attention, pushing prices up is good for the economy.

A Paradelle for Inconsistent Misplacement

Younger than my age, I was born to be inconsistent with the fossil record of our times,
Younger than my age, I was born to be inconsistent with the fossil record of our times,
and misplaced among the artifacts, that spoiled indifference leaves to the labor of tomorrow.
and misplaced among the artifacts, that spoiled indifference leaves to the labor of tomorrow.
Born among the spoiled fossils of indifference ... I was inconsistent with the age of artifacts;
and younger; than the misplaced time to be ... that my labors leave to record our tomorrow.

I'm a throwback from a future so unlike its' past, that today would rather deny it of parenting.
I'm a throwback from a future so unlike its' past, that today would rather deny it of parenting.
Yet here I am, rejected not for who I am, but for what another doesn't want to become.
Yet here I am, rejected not for who I am, but for what another doesn't want to become.
For parenting a future today doesn't want to become ... I'm rejected here, not for who I am,
but from it. Its' throwback past so unlike what another would deny; that I am rather of a yet.

Artificial origins are forgotten in the immediacy of now; I have no history or beginning.
Artificial origins are forgotten in the immediacy of now; I have no history or beginning.
It's simply my fall from what is yet to be, that dumbfounds this cursive notation of time.
It's simply my fall from what is yet to be, that dumbfounds this cursive notation of time.
I have no cursive or forgotten origins that dumbfound artificial history. Yet, what ... in my
notation of this time to be ... is now; simply the beginnings of are fall from it's immediacy?

Born among cursive artifacts that are forgotten of time; I was simply that spoiled throwback;
tomorrow doesn't want yet in now ... or rather I'm the misplaced. I am so unlike here for who
I am. But for times younger than my age, I have no origins to be rejected from what a fossil
would become. Its' not past notation of artificial parenting that dumbfounds today; it's my
immediacy with the future. And yet, our record of a fall from this labor ... what it is to be ...
leaves the indifference of history to ... to deny the inconsistent beginning of another.

A Paradelle for Our Times

Despite the politically prescribed, and promised amounts of mortgaged dreams and false hope,
Despite the politically prescribed, and promised amounts of mortgaged dreams and false hope,
the desperate recipe for turning cheap labor into a renewable form of daylight has failed.
the desperate recipe for turning cheap labor into a renewable form of daylight has failed.
And despite the promised recipe ... and renewable amounts of cheap daylight; the desperate
hope prescribed for politically turning false dreams into a mortgaged form of labor has failed.

Not to be outmaneuvered, by the insistence of our most common temptations and painful circumstances,
Not to be outmaneuvered, by the insistence of our most common temptations and painful circumstances,
the governments of the world have at last acknowledged their determined commitment to cheating fate.
the governments of the world have at last acknowledged their determined commitment to cheating fate.
At the insistence of common fate ... most governments have acknowledged their commitment to cheating
the world. And outmaneuvered by determined circumstances; not to be the last of our painful temptations.

Elsewhere, in the daily drive to undermine the spirit of sincere self disclosure and compromise,
Elsewhere, in the daily drive to undermine the spirit of sincere self disclosure and compromise,
leaders of the western world have admitted ... to their dirty old history of dealing with the devil.
leaders of the western world, have admitted ... to their dirty old history of dealing with the devil.
And with their disclosure of dirty dealing the devil in old world history ... leaders have admitted
to the daily drive of the western elsewhere self; to undermine the spirit of sincere compromise.

Despite the amount of daily compromise the recipes of western history have in their promised temptations
... and the determined drive to a most desperate form of false disclosure ... the self prescribed commitment
mortgaged fate has for cheating hope ... their failed governments of painful labor and cheap circumstances
have at last acknowledged, and admitted; to dealing politically with; and to turning into ... the common devil.
Elsewhere; not to be outmaneuvered by the sincere insistence of daylight;
the dirty dreams of our old world leaders undermine the renewable world of the spirit.

A Paradelle for Dead Meat on a Bun

Dan practiced taxidermy, until he lost his stomach on the gore of fresh killed blood.
Dan practiced taxidermy, until he lost his stomach on the gore of fresh killed blood.
But; he still had an appetite for the public display of dead animals ... what was love to do?
But; he still had an appetite for the public display of dead animals ... what was love to do?
Dan was taxidermy on display until an appetite for gore killed what stomach he still had.
He lost his love to do the fresh blood of animals ... of the public ... but practiced dead.

A pornographic solution revealed itself one night, while waiting in a fast food drive through,
A pornographic solution revealed itself one night, while waiting in a fast food drive through,
the photographs of burgers on buns exited a desire beyond the ordinary norm of salivation.
the photographs of burgers on buns exited a desire beyond the ordinary norm of salivation.
A pornographic food solution revealed itself, through a drive-in desire beyond the photographs
of one-night burgers on fast buns ... the salivation of waiting awhile ... excited ordinary Norm.

But the transformation was immediate, his salvation was found, life never looked so good.
But the transformation was immediate, his salvation was found, life never looked so good.
So, not to be outdone by an undue sensitivity, he would preserve dead meat in living color.
So, not to be outdone by an undue sensitivity, he would preserve dead meat in living color.
Transformation was so due, the good life looked immediate ... but his salvation in sensitivity
was never found. So, not to be out done by dead meat, he would preserve an unliving color.

In his photographs of fresh meat, Dan revealed color beyond what ordinary desire was due.
He would preserve to do so ... until the pornographic gore of dead blood on buns was killed
by salivation. Norman, practiced transformation on fast food; but one night out his stomach
had to be itself ... a good solution was not an immediate display of sensitivity. But in the life
he found while awaiting salvation; the **Drive Through Taxidermy** still exited public appetite
for the undone ... the dead animals never looked so living ... he a ... lost a love of burgers.

45

A Paradelle for: Except for the Small Fact of a Most Particular Matter

Except for the small fact of a most particular matter,
Except for the small fact of a most particular matter,
the future of the worlds happiness and bliss would be assured.
the future of the worlds happiness and bliss would be assured.
And except for the future of the worlds most assured fact;
the particular happiness of bliss would be a small matter.

But who am I to speak with such a certitude, when wiser fools than I disagree.
But who am I to speak with such a certitude, when wiser fools than I disagree.
And why provoke the obvious, when there's nothing to prove other than my own ignorance?
And why provoke the obvious, when there's nothing to prove other than my own ignorance?
But why disagree when the obvious proves wiser than my own certitude? And who am I
to provoke a fool ... when there's nothing other than I ... to speak with such ignorance?

If not for the grace of breath's continuity, the silence of the world would be deafening.
If not for the grace of breath's continuity, the silence of the world would be deafening.
The singularity of death is ... without question ... the last unanswered mystery of life.
The singularity of death is ... without question ... the last unanswered mystery of life.
If not for the ... the unanswered silence of death ... the continuity of the world would
be without grace. Mystery's last question of life, is the deafening singularity of breath.

When such a particular future of happiness is the unanswered fact ... and the ...
the world's last breath questions the certitude of matter ... why disagree with the obvious?
If I speak out for the mystery of grace; when would ignorance not be wiser than most fools?
And who am I ... to provoke a small singularity of life, other than to prove there's nothing
with my own continuity? Except for the deafening silence of death ...
the bliss of the world would be but assured.

A Paradelle for Something to Celebrate

Tomorrow is the anniversary of a bomb that gave birth to a future of unimaginable fear.
Tomorrow is the anniversary of a bomb that gave birth to a future of unimaginable fear.
Today is the birthday of a President who ... who created more ills than the world will ever cure.
Today is the birthday of a President who ... who created more ills than the world will ever cure.
Is ... is the President, who today gave birth to a fear of tomorrow, of more unimaginable ills
than ever ... the birthday anniversary bomb that will cure the created world of a ... a future?

Yesterday promised a solution to a problem that has plagued our minds' since forever.
Yesterday promised a solution to a problem that has plagued our minds' since forever.
But the past remains cluttered with low probabilities; and the fallen hopes of high ideals.
But the past remains cluttered with low probabilities; and the fallen hopes of high ideals.
But since that promised yesterday cluttered our minds' with high hopes and fallen ideals
... a low probabilities past, has forever plagued the remains of a solution to the problem.

In the moment passing; and preceding this one, time stood still on the edge of annihilation.
In the moment passing; and preceding this one, time stood still on the edge of annihilation.
But with a soft sigh of relief; the continuity of breath returned life's celebration to itself.
But with a soft sigh of relief; the continuity of breath returned life's celebration to itself.
In the moment preceding the celebration ... this one soft sigh of itself ... stood life's breath
on the edge of still relief, and returned to continuity with but a passing annihilation of time.

But since the high solution of a low probabilities President is to a ... bomb the problem,
our fallen ideals stood the world on edge. And with that: today's cure is a birthday of fear
tomorrow promised relief yesterday ... and gave more cluttered hope to a future plagued
with ills than the anniversary of a past ever will. But who ... created this continuity of one
unimaginable moment? That in the celebration preceding the annihilation of itself, life's
breath has returned to the birth of time? The soft sigh's passing of a still mind remains forever.

a paradelle for an upstart thief

ego is the upstart thief of the Self, claiming all qualities of the conscious soul as its own,
ego is the upstart thief of the Self, claiming all qualities of the conscious soul as its own,
corrupting the purpose and spirit of our lives in the glorification of itself is vain arrogance.
corrupting the purpose and spirit of our lives in the glorification of itself is vain arrogance.
in claiming the vain thief as itself, the upstart ego, is its own corrupting arrogance. the soul
purpose of our lives ... is glorification of spirit; and of all the qualities of the conscious Self.

assuming the status of the historical center of all significance, in existence and of time,
assuming the status of the historical center of all significance, in existence and of time,
the I of an unblinking identity is blind to the fluid radiance of an ever present eternity.
the I of an unblinking identity is blind to the fluid radiance of an ever present eternity.
the unblinking radiance of, of all existence ... assuming the present center and historical
status of the significance of an I in time ... is blind to the eternity of an ever fluid identity.

stealing conscience away from our hearts, and confiscating the wisdom of consciousness,
stealing conscience away from our hearts, and confiscating the wisdom of consciousness,
the soul and the embrace of its breath are buried beneath layers of conquest and conceit.
the soul and the embrace of its breath are buried beneath layers of conquest and conceit.
stealing away the breath, and the soul of consciousness from our hearts; layers of wisdom
and conscience are buried beneath the conceit of conquest, and its confiscating embrace.

the fluid radiance in our hearts and the embrace of eternity; the wisdom center of the soul
and all qualities of conscience ... are buried beneath layers of historical time. and stealing
away the soul status of the ever present Self ... and ... and claiming Itself as an unblinking
glorification of the significance of conceit; the ego is confiscating an I of conscious purpose
from the breath of all existence ...is the assuming identity of its own upstart arrogance ...
is the corrupting thief, blind to the spirit of our lives, in its vain conquest of consciousness.

A Paradelle for a Day on the Lake

In the morning calm before the wind, sitting at the beachside café, eating bacon and eggs ...
In the morning calm before the wind, sitting at the beachside café, eating bacon and eggs ...
passing clouds imperceptibly pause to observe themselves in the still surface of the lake.
passing clouds imperceptibly pause to observe themselves in the still surface of the lake.
Beachside in the café, eating eggs and bacon ... the morning clouds, imperceptibly passing
wind; pause at the surface to observe themselves; before sitting still in the calm of the lake.

Ancient volcanoes stand silent, in humble witness to their own clear and reflected sentience.
Ancient volcanoes stand silent, in humble witness to their own clear and reflected sentience.
In the village below; an afternoon sun, sidewalk vendors, stone streets, and a four beer lunch.
In the village below; an afternoon sun, sidewalk vendors, stone streets, and a four beer lunch.
In sun reflected streets below silent volcanoes; stand four sidewalk vendors in stone witness
to an ancient sentience and their own humble lunch ... the village beer and a clear afternoon.

A walk through town, down to the wooden boat docks, where shining lights surround the water.
A walk through town, down to the wooden boat docks, where shining lights surround the water.
An evening bell sings a prayer; to a row of taco stands, popular and illuminated in the night.
An evening bell sings a prayer; to a row of taco stands, popular and illuminated in the night.
An evening walk to the town bell; where a popular, illuminated taco stands shining into the night.
Lights surround a wooden boat ... and down a row of docks ... prayer sings through the water.

The morning boat docks in at a popular village café. Sitting down to four beachside volcanoes
... bacon and eggs ... and the illuminated calm ... the still water of the lake reflected a sentience;
shining below the surface. Clouds passing in the wind, pause to observe and humble themselves
before an ancient stone ... where sidewalk vendors ... stand silent in the clear afternoon sun ...
imperceptibly eating their own lunch. And through the streets ... in witness to an evening walk;
beer lights surround a row of wooden taco stands ... town bells sing a prayer into the night.

A Paradelle for Unexplainable Prescience

In the event of a sudden time shift; Art kept fresh sealed chocolate bars stuffed in his pockets.
In the event of a sudden time shift; Art kept fresh sealed chocolate bars stuffed in his pockets.
Time traveling future or past, the food of the gods is a great way to make new friends.
Time traveling future or past, the food of the gods is a great way to make new friends.
Is the event of gods chocolate bars, time traveling past the fresh sealed future kept stuffed
in his pockets ... the new way in food, a sudden shift of friends, or a time to make great art?

In preparation, he would imagine it happening; envisioning the encounters in his mind.
In preparation, he would imagine it happening; envisioning the encounters in his mind.
The future possible occurrence of traveling back through time required avoiding conflict.
The future possible occurrence of traveling back through time required avoiding conflict.
Avoiding the encounters required preparation in his mind. Envisioning possible conflict,
he would imagine traveling back through the future occurrence of it happening in time.

In retrospect, it *was* an odd sight, to a ... see himself exist outside the known flow of time.
In retrospect, it *was* an odd sight, to a ... see himself exist outside the known flow of time.
But there he was, standing behind himself, moments away from where he would be or ... was?
But there he was, standing behind himself, moments away from where he would be or ... was?
He was moments away from standing there, an odd himself outside of a known himself,
he was retrospect to exist behind where the flow in time would be, but was it sight or see?

To make the future exist required envisioning odd moments stuffed away in known pockets of time.
Was it the time in his mind traveling past himself or ... or in retrospect ... great gods' possible future?
Standing in preparation ... outside the sight of time. ... he would imagine there was a way to see
a conflict. In a sudden occurrence of himself, he is traveling back from where he ... an Art event
was happening. It sealed the time shift through food. But, his friends kept avoiding
the would be new encounters behind the flow of fresh chocolate bars.

A Paradelle for the Sun is Melting

There is no doubt that the sun is melting into space, but no one's been able to prove it.
There is no doubt that the sun is melting into space, but no one's been able to prove it.
Silent as the moon in her full-reflected glory, this secret of the sun remains its own.
Silent as the moon in her full-reflected glory, this secret of the sun remains its own.
No one's been into the no space of this secret sun; but there, its moon is able to prove
that in her own full glory ... the melting doubt remains reflected ... as the silent sun it is.

Slowly succumbing to the vacuum of space, vaporizing into the nothingness of now,
Slowly succumbing to the vacuum of space, vaporizing into the nothingness of now,
no less radiant in its vanishing glow, than the clouds above the dawn of light's horizon.
no less radiant in its vanishing glow, than the clouds above the dawn of light's horizon.
In the vacuum of now ... of radiant space succumbing no less ... than to the glow above
its horizon ... the dawn of slowly vaporizing into nothingness lights the vanishing clouds.

Let not the brilliance of the moon be its measure, the moon fades and precisely returns.
Let not the brilliance of the moon be its measure, the moon fades and precisely returns.
As for the declining mass of erratic vibrations in a stationary sun ... it's not the same void.
As for the declining mass of erratic vibrations in a stationary sun ... it's not the same void.
The precisely declining moon fades and returns as the same moon. Let not a stationary
measure of vibrations be the brilliance of the erratic void; for in its mass; it's not the sun.

The sun fades no less, into it's own space, than slowly succumbing to the nothingness
of melting clouds. Now that the reflected moon is a stationary mass; there is no doubt
in the measure of her glory. But as of this, the secret brilliance of the sun remains silent,
and no one's been able to prove precisely; it's not ... in it's full glow ... dawn's radiant light.
As for the moon, the moon returns in the declining vacuum of its vibrations. Let it not be
the same erratic void of the sun ... vanishing into space ... vaporizing above the horizon.

A Paradelle for Being the Was I Wasn't

If a ... there ever was a once there was, then I haven't been the has been I could have been.
If a ... there ever was a once there was, then I haven't been the has been I could have been.
And who could I be, but the otherwise person pretending to be the I he was that wasn't.
And who could I be, but the otherwise person pretending to be the I he was that wasn't.
Wasn't the I that was pretending to be the I who could be, the I he could have otherwise been?
But if ever there was a person ... and once there was ... then I haven't been a has been.

But I would still be someone who I wasn't, if I wasn't busy becoming a being who never was.
But I would still be someone who I wasn't, if I wasn't busy becoming a being who never was.
After all, if I couldn't be anyone other than who I possibly am, I wouldn't be who I fully was.
After all, if I couldn't be anyone other than who I possibly am, I wouldn't be who I fully was.
But who wouldn't I be ... if I wasn't someone who was still ... a ... if I was? I couldn't possibly be
busy being who I wasn't. After all, I would never be anyone other than who I am fully becoming.

I am a living making of myself, I've left behind the worn out currency of a would be wanna be,
I am a living making of myself, I've left behind the worn out currency of a would be wanna be,
the makeshift counterfeit identity of the economic self, a being whose true value has been had.
the makeshift counterfeit identity of the economic self, a being whose true value has been had.
Myself, I've left behind the economic value of a counterfeit identity, whose worn out wanna be
self had the makeshift making of a has been. I am a living would be, the true currency of being.

But I wouldn't be the currency of who I am ... if I had never left the counterfeit once who was behind.
I would still be busy being a worn out has been ... whose true identity wasn't who I could have been.
I was a could be, there I've been, if I was ... the then and there economic wanna be of a haven't ever
been pretending to be I was but otherwise ... a makeshift self ... making myself a would be someone
who wasn't the person that he was. After all, if I wasn't the living value a becoming being has ...
I couldn't fully ... possibly be ... the I of anyone other than who I am.

A Paradelle for ... One Hand Clapping

If one hand clapping held no mirror, how would we ever be able to see our original face?
If one hand clapping held no mirror, how would we ever be able to see our original face?
Textured as the moon in its witness of time, transparent as the air surrounding our breath.
Textured as the moon in its witness of time, transparent as the air surrounding our breath.
If we hand held our able mirror, to see the textured face of our original witness ... its breath ...
how would air surrounding the moon ever be as transparent as no one clapping in time?

Given our distance from the obvious; the nothingness of eternity has no name, no beginning.
Given our distance from the obvious; the nothingness of eternity has no name, no beginning.
In the bamboo forest, the evening sky lingers upon the horizon, absorbing itself into darkness.
In the bamboo forest, the evening sky lingers upon the horizon, absorbing itself into darkness.
From no obvious beginning; the distance lingers upon itself in the evening sky. Absorbing the
horizon into the no name forest; darkness has given our nothingness the eternity of bamboo.

Meditating in silence, Buddha ... met a man with no head. Could nirvana ever be nearer than now?
Meditating in silence, Buddha ... met a man with no head. Could nirvana ever be nearer than now?
Clouds pass by unconvincingly. A lone bird, sailing on the breeze, disappears into the radiant void.
Clouds pass by unconvincingly. A lone bird, sailing on the breeze, disappears into the radiant void.
Unconvincingly ... a head disappears into a man with no void. Buddha met nirvana by meditating in
radiant silence. Could clouds ever pass nearer the breeze, than the lone bird now sailing be ... on?

Clapping itself unconvincingly, one hand disappears into silence. Given our beginning in nothingness;
could the radiant face, now absorbing our original void; ever be as obvious as the man in the moon?
How would we ever be able to see a forest, pass from the Buddha horizon into the no name sky ...
if nirvana lingers no nearer than a bird in the distance; sailing by on transparent clouds of time?
Meditating upon our witness of the lone no ... textured evening air met with the bamboo breeze,
darkness held its head ... the breath surrounding eternity has no mirror.

A Paradelle ... But for the Labor of Trees

Holding space between earth and sky, a magnificent silence permeates our measure of time,
Holding space between earth and sky, a magnificent silence permeates our measure of time,
each moment suspended, easily through the air, connecting to the next one, until all become one.
each moment suspended, easily through the air, connecting to the next one, until all become one.
Holding time between earth and sky, a suspended silence easily permeates each moment of our
measure ... until, through the air connecting one to the next, all become one magnificent space.

Groaning with the weight of the wind, roots grasping for rocks, as limbs are blown in disarray;
Groaning with the weight of the wind, roots grasping for rocks, as limbs are blown in disarray;
leaves scatter in the breeze, scrambling over the hillside, each crumbling into the dust lost beneath us.
leaves scatter in the breeze, scrambling over the hillside, each crumbling into the dust lost beneath us.
Beneath the limbs groaning for the weight lost in the breeze, roots in disarray scatter rocks over
the hillside, as grasping leaves are blown scrambling with the wind, crumbling each of us into dust.

Standing in stillness, observing, unnoticed, trees reveal themselves as the unseen soul of the world;
Standing in stillness, observing, unnoticed, trees reveal themselves as the unseen soul of the world;
their sentient beingness labors in the realm of spirit, unwitnessed; rejoicing and radiant in the rain.
their sentient beingness labors in the realm of spirit, unwitnessed; rejoicing and radiant in the rain.
And as radiant spirit labors in the unwitnessed world, rejoicing unnoticed in the realm of beingness,
trees ... observing themselves standing in the rain, reveal the unseen stillness of their sentient soul.

Standing beneath the weight of a world in disarray ... limbs; grasping for rocks the earth suspended
into space; trees, rejoicing in the sentient air reveal the breeze, groaning unnoticed through the sky.
Their labors are in observing, over one hillside and to the next, unseen roots connecting easily with
the wind blown rain; as leaves scatter themselves in the crumbling realm between silence and dust.
Until ... holding the lost soul in each of us ... as all become the stillness of the one radiant spirit;
magnificent beingness permeates each unwitnessed moment; scrambling our measure of time.

A Paradelle for Being Small Minded

Within this ever-expanding universe, nobody's world is big enough for being small minded,
Within this ever-expanding universe, nobody's world is big enough for being small minded,
contracting out of ignorance and fear into the one-dimensional self-enclosure of the lone ego.
contracting out of ignorance and fear into the one-dimensional self-enclosure of the lone ego.
Within the fear minded universe of lone self ignorance ... this ego, expanding out of nobody's
ever contracting world and into the big enclosure; is small enough for being one-dimensional.

Living a life defined by public opinion, defending the beliefs of others as if they were one's own,
Living a life defined by public opinion, defending the beliefs of others as if they were one's own,
the vanity of conditioning reflexively contains curiosity, from ever encountering an open mind.
the vanity of conditioning reflexively contains curiosity, from ever encountering an open mind.
Living as if others were defending the public from ever encountering the mind of an open life ...
they defined curiosity by a vanity of opinion. One's own conditioning reflexively contains beliefs.

Without question; the most common error of ignorance begins in the pride of a thoughtless mind,
Without question; the most common error of ignorance begins in the pride of a thoughtless mind,
living its life as an invented story, inflated with a false sense of self, empty of any ideas of its own.
living its life as an invented story, inflated with a false sense of self, empty of any ideas of its own.
With the error of an invented self, as the most common sense of, of its own thoughtless ignorance,
a mind empty of its story ... without any false ideas of inflated pride; begins a life living in question.

Open minded with others, a living being contains this big universe of mind. The ego ... expanding
out of a lone opinion in the ignorance of pride ... inflated within the self enclosure of public beliefs,
begins its own thoughtless life as an empty question. Its as if they were false nobody's defending
any small enough sense of self living without curiosity ... an ignorance defined by a story of error,
forever contracting from the world of mind ... and into the most common fear of ever encountering
one's own ideas. Vanity ... the conditioning of invented life ... is reflexively one-dimensional.

A Paradelle for the Greatest Illusion

The greatest illusion is that we can free others of their suffering through our own liberation.
The greatest illusion is that we can free others of their suffering through our own liberation.
In truth, we can only save them from the pain of our own unconscious fear-based behaviors.
In truth, we can only save them from the pain of our own unconscious fear-based behaviors.
Our greatest truth is based in fear, the illusion that we can save others from the pain of their
own unconscious behaviors. Through liberation, we can only free them of our own suffering.

But, we either imprison ourselves in the drama of misery, hiding behind a curse for being born.
But, we either imprison ourselves in the drama of misery, hiding behind a curse for being born,
or we struggle to escape from suffering by opposing it, calling for its end as if it were a disease.
or we struggle to escape from suffering by opposing it, calling for its end as if it were a disease.
But ... in opposing the struggle to escape hiding it from ourselves ... we either imprison suffering
behind a drama of calling for its end, or we curse it for being, as if misery were born by a disease.

Sadly, we remain ignorant of what suffering can teach us, oblivious to the wisdom it can bring.
Sadly, we remain ignorant of what suffering can teach us, oblivious to the wisdom it can bring.
In fact, our denial in the purpose of pain perpetuates the unending tragedy of life on earth.
In fact, our denial in the purpose of pain perpetuates the unending tragedy of life on earth.
The pain of denial perpetuates our ignorant suffering. In fact, we remain oblivious of what life
on the earth can teach us. Sadly ... it can bring unending tragedy into the purpose of wisdom.

We teach ourselves to remain oblivious of the purpose behind life ... by opposing it for what it is
... our own struggle through ignorant suffering. The pain of tragedy only perpetuates the illusion
that escape-based drama can free us of the misery of unconscious behaviors. But can we end it?
Can liberation? Can we save our own wisdom from ... from hiding in a fear of the fact of suffering?
Sadly, in calling suffering our pain for being born ... we either bring others into unending denial,
or we imprison them in their greatest curse on earth ... it's as if the truth were a disease.

A Paradelle for One Devil ... Many Gods

Does it matter how you worship god, or even what god you worship, if it's always the same old devil?
Does it matter how you worship god, or even what god you worship, if it's always the same old devil?
I mean; if it is the same old devil, then it would appear that no religion by itself can succeed him.
I mean; if it is the same old devil, then it would appear that no religion by itself can succeed him.
I mean it ... if you always worship god by what god you worship, does it matter then ... that no religion
can succeed itself; if it ... it's devil is the same old him? Or even how the same old devil would appear?

If the demons we see in ourselves and each other are imaginary, how real can the devil himself be?
If the demons we see in ourselves and each other are imaginary, how real can the devil himself be?
I mean, if all good people of god's faith are out fighting the devil ... why are they killing each other?
I mean, if all good people of god's faith are out fighting the devil ... why are they killing each other?
We see in ourselves how the real devil can be himself. I mean ... if good people are gods imaginary
devil ... why are the demons, if they are all the faith of each other, out fighting and killing each other?

With so many false gods outside of us, each one claiming to be the one and only true god inside of us,
With so many false gods outside of us, each one claiming to be the one and only true god inside of us,
it doesn't take that much of a devil within us to prove more powerful than any idea of a god without.
it doesn't take that much of a devil within us to prove more powerful than any idea of a god without.
Without one true one and only within us ... with so many false gods; each claiming to be more powerful
than any idea of a devil inside of us ... it doesn't take that much of a god to prove the god outside of us.

It doesn't take that much of a religion to bedevil the same old him in each of us. I mean it ... if the god
you worship is always claiming to be real by fighting the same old imaginary demons, why does the faith
of so many good people appear more powerful than god himself? I mean ... if no god or devil can succeed
itself without killing us ... can it matter then ... if within each god's one true devil, all other gods are false?
And even if you prove it ... how would anyone see that without the idea of a devil inside of ourselves;
we are only what god ... and the devil outside us are ... it's how they worship each other.

A Paradelle for Reincarnation and Life Insurance

Frank lost his life insurance, when a random survey revealed that he believed in ... in reincarnation.
Frank lost his life insurance, when a random survey revealed that he believed in ... in reincarnation.
Nothing he had ever experienced before ... or in the past; prepared him for the shock and disbelief.
Nothing he had ever experienced before ... or in the past; prepared him for the shock and disbelief.
Nothing that he had ever believed in or before, prepared him for the survey. And when he revealed
his frank disbelief in ... in random reincarnation ... a past life experienced the lost insurance shock.

Apparently, for anyone who has lived and died more than once, death is a pre-existing condition.
Apparently, for anyone who has lived and died more than once, death is a pre-existing condition.
It is after all, an agreement made in good faith, that once the insured dies, that they will remain dead.
It is after all, an agreement made in good faith, that once the insured dies, that they will remain dead.
An agreement that once lived in faith has died. Apparently they [the insured good and dead] made it
a pre-condition, for existing after death. All that will remain is ... is anyone who dies more than once.

However, if one can provide the proper documentation from the ethereal record of souls department,
However, if one can provide the proper documentation from the ethereal record of souls department,
clearly confirming that your own soul is in fact your one and only soul ... the policy can be reinstated.
clearly confirming that your own soul is in fact your one and only soul ... the policy can be reinstated.
However, only the soul of souls, from documentation department one ... can provide the proper record
confirming that if your own soul is clearly, and in fact the one ... your ethereal policy can be reinstated.

Frankly, a policy that he only lived once, had him preparing for nothing more than the documentation.
After all, once death is reinstated ... your souls faith in the agreement can remain in shock. In fact ...
they believed that made it clear ... if your own soul is lost in the random past department ... and one dies
before the survey ... the insured pre-dead will provide a proper insurance record for anyone who has died
 ... in, of ... and or from ... disbelief. However ... his reincarnation revealed an apparently existing condition;
and one that he confirmed ... that whenever the ethereal soul can be experienced ... life is good.

A Paradelle for Grave Reservations

In being a, a fatalist; Doug had grave reservations whenever he made a decision about his future.
In being a, a fatalist; Doug had grave reservations whenever he made a decision about his future.
But what he had in his mind when he thought about it, was nothing less, if not larger than, his life.
But what he had in his mind when he thought about it, was nothing less, if not larger than, his life.
But, if nothing he thought about in his mindless indecision had a future when not being a fatalist ...
whenever it was what he had his reservations about; Doug a ... he made his grave larger than life.

After all, given the choice to decide ... between one's own fulfillment and what must and can only be,
After all, given the choice to decide ... between one's own fulfillment and what must and can only be,
he knew that he'd be fooling no one else but himself; if he even dreamed he could choose the former.
he knew that he'd be fooling no one else but himself; if he even dreamed he could choose the former.
Given to fooling himself if he could ... even he knew; that after he'd dreamed the former, the fulfillment
he choose must be ... be but between what no one else can decide, and one's own all and only choice.

But he was uncomfortable with the promise of life, and preferred instead to fear for the end of each day,
But he was uncomfortable with the promise of life, and preferred instead to fear for the end of each day,
tomorrow has been and will always be, at its best on any given day, an unsafe and insecure proposition.
tomorrow has been and will always be, at its best on any given day, an unsafe and insecure proposition.
But he was given instead to an insecure fear of life; and on any day, and each day, uncomfortable at best.
The proposition preferred for tomorrow will be, and has always been ... with the end of its unsafe promise.

He dreamed he could choose in his mind, each future and former self; but Doug, he made a grave decision.
He knew, that when given the choice between nothing at its best, and a lifeless proposition, he'd be no one
else but him; if he was into fooling about being a fatalist. But even when he thought to decide for the safe
unfulfillment he had with his will ... had it not always been about what was, and must be, an uncomfortable
fear? And after all ... if instead ... on any given day ... one's own and only preferred tomorrow has insecure
reservations, what promise of the day can ever be larger than the end of his life?

A Paradelle for Jasmine Rose

Her breath was like a bench press, forcing itself from her mouth ... hissing against her tight trembling lips.
Her breath was like a bench press, forcing itself from her mouth ... hissing against her tight trembling lips.
Jasmine Rose was doing her best not to smell like an old sweaty towel, left in the bottom of a, a gym bag.
Jasmine Rose was doing her best not to smell like an old sweaty towel, left in the bottom of a, a gym bag.
Bench breath left itself a smell in her mouth; forcing Rose to press her lips. Her best towel sweaty against
the bottom of her ... Ana was like, hissing from doing gym. Jasmine, trembling like a tight old bag, was not.

She was struggling to lift her own weight clothed, while dressed like a cowgirl, pommeling off on a horse.
She was struggling to lift her own weight clothed, while dressed like a cowgirl, pommeling off on a horse.
Not in her wildest dreams, did she ever imagine herself, being so driven to succeed, so determined to win.
Not in her wildest dreams, did she ever imagine herself, being so driven to succeed, so determined to win.
She was like a struggling cowgirl determined to lift herself off her own horse. Pommeling to a weight driven
win while dressed in her wildest dreams ... she did not imagine ever being so on ... so clothed to succeed.

A cheer rose up from the crowd, she planted her feet, and turned 3 circles; before grunting like a shot put.
A cheer rose up from the crowd, she planted her feet, and turned 3 circles; before grunting like a shot put.
After all it wasn't like she was doing a dead lift, she had momentum beneath her, she carried herself away.
After all it wasn't like she was doing a dead lift, she had momentum beneath her, she carried herself away.
Before her lift turned up shot, she put circles beneath a planted rose. Grunting like a ... she had 3 dead feet;
like all her momentum wasn't doing it, and she was after a cheer ... she carried herself away from the crowd.

Clothed like a cowgirl ... Roseana planted herself on a grunting horse. A cheer rose up from the bottom
of her feet. Jasmine; she was like, dressed in a sweaty old towel; trembling beneath her own dead weight.
She was doing her wildest bench press, while struggling to lift the crowd against her tight determined lips.
Her mouth left 3 circles hissing in a bag she carried ... forcing her breath not to imagine itself ... ever being
so driven from her dreams. After all, she did not like gym and pommeling a win wasn't doing it. So, her best
shot to succeed herself; before she was put away like a turned off lift; was to smell like she had momentum.

A Paradelle for Three Peters

One day while out saving the world from its problems, Peter was confronted by a pissed off panhandler.
One day while out saving the world from its problems, Peter was confronted by a pissed off panhandler.
But he was all out of pocket change ... and felt reluctant to give the man the ten-dollar bill he demanded.
But he was all out of pocket change ... and felt reluctant to give the man the ten-dollar bill he demanded.
The reluctant giver felt confronted while saving the day from its problems. He was out of pocket by a one
dollar bill. But Peter Pan ... demanded the ten. He was all pissed off; and out to manhandle world change.

The man put Peter off; his day had been great until called into account for the change he hadn't made;
The man put Peter off; his day had been great until called into account for the change he hadn't made;
Despite all of his efforts, the exchange seemed to be going nowhere; all he wanted to do was disappear.
Despite all of his efforts, the exchange seemed to be going nowhere; all he wanted to do was disappear.
Until, Peter the Great had change put into his account of man ... the called exchange hadn't been made
for the day off he wanted. Despite all his efforts to be going nowhere, all he seemed to do was disappear.

Peter pondered his predicament ... it appeared to be the time to pull the proverbial rabbit out of his hat.
Peter pondered his predicament ... it appeared to be the time to pull the proverbial rabbit out of his hat.
He had been so obsessed with saving the souls of everyone else, he had conveniently forgotten himself.
He had been so obsessed with saving the souls of everyone else, he had conveniently forgotten himself.
To pull himself out of the predicament; Peter conveniently pondered the obsessed soul of everyone else.
His rabbits had been so proverbial with saving the time; it appeared to be he ... he had forgotten his hat.

Peter Pan appeared obsessed with saving himself from time change ... until one day ... despite the all out
efforts of Peter the Great ... the ten dollar bill his pocket pondered confronted his reluctant account handler.
His predicament? He had conveniently forgotten to give the man, the change he hadn't been for the world.
So while the man demanded he call off the exchange of the souls output ... everyone else was pissed off
by going nowhere. And Peter Rabbit? All he wanted was to be pulled out!!! He had seemed to be saving
his day of all of its problems; he had been proverbial to do it ... but was made to disappear into a felt hat.

A Paradelle for a Pre-Reprehensible Tale

Before the blame gets passed around for the current conditions in our country, we must exercise a caution.
Before the blame gets passed around for the current conditions in our country, we must exercise a caution.
Especially, when greed breeds like a disease, and politicians profit themselves by exposing us to danger.
Especially, when greed breeds like a disease, and politicians profit themselves by exposing us to danger.
A caution: before a disease like blame gets passed around ... and especially when greed breeds conditions
for profit; we the country; must exercise current US politicians, by exposing them to the danger in ourselves.

Based on inflation, the market driven purchase price for an elected official remains a durable investment.
Based on inflation, the market driven purchase price for an elected official remains a durable investment.
Fluid in the fine art of selling confidence in false hope; even in the best of times ... random shit can happen.
Fluid in the fine art of selling confidence in false hope; even in the best of times ... random shit can happen.
In the fine shit selling, inflation driven investment market ... an official purchase remains elected for a price.
Even in ... in times of random hope, based on the fluid art of false confidence; the durable best can happen.

To gain the proper grasp on the situation; to apprehend its gravity, and not be left hanging by our asses ...
To gain the proper grasp on the situation; to apprehend its gravity, and not be left hanging by our asses ...
we need to stand our ground in demanding that our public servants serve our interest and not their own.
we need to stand our ground in demanding that our public servants serve our interest and not their own.
In demanding that our grasp not public servants apprehend their own asses ... we need to stand and serve,
and not be left hanging by the gravity of the situation. It's our ... to our interest ... to gain our proper ground.

When price driven profit breeds disease-like conditions in our politicians, especially the servants elected to
serve our country and not themselves; we caution the situation before a proper danger gets passed around.
We need to exercise a durable and fluid confidence in our current grasp to apprehend false gravity, and not be
left hanging by our blame. Even in the times of random shit on ... on the ground ... the hope that remains
must stand in its own best interest. In the public art of selling their fine official asses ... can the purchase
happen for our gain ... by exposing us to a greed based ... inflation demanding for'an investment market?

A Paradelle for Time and Place

Al lived in Seattle, so every day at the same time and place, he took a photograph of the Space Needle.
Al lived in Seattle, so every day at the same time and place, he took a photograph of the Space Needle.
His goal was to capture the ever-changing environmental moods of a famous architectural monument.
His goal was to capture the ever-changing environmental moods of a famous architectural monument.
To capture a goal ever so changing: of the same place Seattle and the environment he lived in ... Al took
a space-time photograph of his architectural moods ... every day at the famous needle was monumental.

Every year at the same date and time, June and Ray re-consecrate their vowels in the same hotel room.
Every year at the same date and time, June and Ray re-consecrate their vowels in the same hotel room.
Oh! Oou! Ah! They sigh and they sing, as two and as one, until neither one, can utter a single consonant.
Oh! Oou! Ah! They sigh and they sing, as two and as one, until neither one, can utter a single consonant.
June and Ray ... date at a **Year One** hotel room... they sing and sigh ... as two in time ... one and the same,
they re-utter every single ah, oh and oou; until neither can, as their vowels consecrate the same consonant.

Breathless on the abyss, Carol always came back to celebrate the Summer Solstice in the Grand Canyon,
Breathless on the abyss, Carol always came back to celebrate the Summer Solstice in the Grand Canyon,
and to witness the variable Moon at sunset, recording in her minds eye its phase and position in the sky.
and to witness the variable Moon at sunset, recording in her minds eye its phase and position in the sky.
Back in the grand canyon, recording the summer moon; Carol always came to celebrate the abyss in her
minds eye. And to witness; on the Solstice in the sky; its breathless phase and variable position at sunset.

Every summer at the *Same Time, Same Place* hotel in Seattle; Carol came to witness, and to sing at sunset,
the ah, oh, oou, environmental moods of the Space Needle ... her vowels breathless on the monument.
Al lived in a photograph he took of the Grand Canyon. The goal was to re-capture his minds variable eye ...
one as two and neither as one ... and consecrate the year and moon time ... so single; and always in phase.
And every Solstice ... in a ... a famous June day recording date ... they can celebrate its ray the sky and sigh.
Until back at the room, in their ever changing abyss position; they utter the same architectural consonant.

A Paradelle for Social Organization

Let's say you want to do a study on social organization, and you decide to begin, with a sewer full of rats.
Let's say you want to do a study on social organization, and you decide to begin, with a sewer full of rats.
Would you start your research with the focus on their nocturnal behaviors, or their appetite for bad press?
Would you start your research with the focus on their nocturnal behaviors, or their appetite for bad press?
Let's say, you decide to press on for the full organization of their social appetite ... do you begin your study
with a rats bad behaviors ... or would you want to start with a nocturnal research, and focus on their sewer?

Now it's common in the study of rats to misinterpret their nuzzling instinct as an expression of affection.
Now it's common in the study of rats to misinterpret their nuzzling instinct as an expression of affection.
That's a mistake; because as we all know, once a rat has gained your confidence; your ass is Swiss cheese.
That's a mistake; because as we all know, once a rat has gained your confidence; your ass is Swiss cheese.
Now as we all know, it's a common mistake to misinterpret Swiss rats. That's because once a rat has your
confidence in the study of their cheese nuzzling instinct ... your ass is gained as an expression of affection.

Mutually dependant relationships; are of course the fundamental structures to the integrity of any society.
Mutually dependant relationships; are of course the fundamental structures to the integrity of any society;
and rats are no exception, save for their slanderous reputation for being the first ones to abandon a sinking ship.
and rats are no exception, save for their slanderous reputation for being the first ones to abandon a sinking ship.
Save for their reputations, being the mutual integrity structures to first abandon the ships course for a society
of fundamental exception, the dependent rats are sinking slanderously and are of no relationship to any one.

With a full expression of commonly bad behaviors, let's say it's a mistake to focus your research on a rats ass.
In the slanderous society of Swiss rats, their appetite for sewer cheese has no press. That's mutual, because
rats with the reputation for sinking a ship, are now the study of the first ones to abandon fundamental structures.
And as we do know, once you begin to misinterpret their exception as a gained relationship ... your confidence
starts being dependant on their nocturnal nuzzling. All you are is their rat ... or would an instinct decide to save
your integrity? And of course ... to study the social organization of any affection you want?

A Paradelle for Human Beings and Chimpanzees

A human being and a chimpanzee, share something like 98 percent plus of the same genetic material;
A human being and a chimpanzee, share something like 98 percent plus of the same genetic material;
yet there are people who deny the similarity ... claiming that a human being is a unique creation of god.
yet there are people who deny the similarity ... claiming that a human being is a unique creation of god.
Being of the same creation ... a chimpanzee is something like 98 percent the who of a human similarity.
And yet there are people, denying a material human being ... that share a unique plus god genetic claim.

Certain traits have humanized well; becoming admirable qualities, but the basic beast remains the same.
Certain traits have humanized well; becoming admirable qualities, but the basic beast remains the same.
And it is our denial of this most observable and self evident fact, that perpetuates suffering in our lives.
And it is our denial of this most observable and self evident fact, that perpetuates suffering in our lives.
The same, well humanized, observable beast, perpetuates our admirable self; and remains evident in it.
But this denial that our basic lives have qualities and traits, is becoming the most certain fact of suffering.

We can bring healing to this ancient wound through our own experience of becoming more fully human;
We can bring healing to this ancient wound through our own experience of becoming more fully human;
embracing within ourselves and each other, our primary and essential need, to be loved, nurtured and secure.
embracing within ourselves and each other, our primary and essential need, to be loved, nurtured and secure.
Can we bring healing to this ancient and essential other; and embracing our own wound, secure our primary
need of becoming more nurtured and loved ... to be fully within ourselves, through each human experience?

Claiming our humanized similarity lives well; ninety eight percent plus of the same essential people; who deny
that god remains within the genetic experience of a chimpanzee, need to be nurtured. Being loved is the most
basic something we can have and share. And yet, there are certain unique human qualities like ... self denial;
that perpetuates our primary wound. But becoming more of a ... a human being ... through our own healing;
bring this ancient human suffering ... and evident, fully observable beast ... to a material fact ... and it is this,
our embracing; and becoming ... the same secure creation, of admirable traits, in ourselves and each other.

A Paradelle for Peace

For God's sake, be your own Jesus; forgive *others* of their ignorance and the suffering that it caused *you.*
For God's sake, be your own Jesus; forgive *others* of their ignorance and the suffering that it caused *you.*
Resist the temptation to blame them for your sorrow. Don't judge *others* for their sins; *do* not hate them.
Resist the temptation to blame them for your sorrow. Don't judge *others* for their sins; *do* not hate them.
And to you others, that hate them others ... for your own sake, don't be the sorrow for their Jesus. *Do* not
judge your sins; forgive them for their ignorance of God's suffering. Resist the blame it caused temptation.

In the name of Allah, peace be *unto you,* who open your heart *as* did Muhammad, in his surrender to god.
In the name of Allah, peace be *unto you,* who open your heart *as* did Muhammad, in his surrender to god.
Embrace the truth god has given *unto* you. *Would* it be the work or a word, praise and proclaim His mercy.
Embrace the truth god has given *unto* you. *Would* it be the work or a word, praise and proclaim His mercy.
Be open *unto* the embrace of God, or surrender your heart to work in peace. Be it the God who has given
unto you his truth; *would* you praise His mercy in a word, *as* did Muhammad; and proclaim the name Allah?

Open your eyes as Moses and behold the Spirit of the Lord; deliver yourself from hatred and its captivity.
Open your eyes as Moses and behold the Spirit of the Lord; deliver yourself from hatred and its captivity.
Let your conscience be a nation of justice for those who *have* none, *do* not hold others in fear, release them.
Let your conscience be a nation of justice for those who *have* none, *do* not hold others in fear, release them.
And as Moses, release your eyes from fear and behold the captivity of a nation. Let the spirit of conscience
be your Lord. Open yourself in those others who do not have its justice. Hold hatred for none. Deliver them.

Do not surrender your heart **unto** a hatred. Work to forgive **others, as you** deliver them from the sorrow
that caused your blame. **Would** you embrace none of them in the spirit of your Lord? Be it for Moses, Jesus,
for Allah and his Muhammad; release the suffering nation of your sins and proclaim peace! Don't hate the fear
for its captivity; **have** your open eyes be god's praise! Be it for **others,** His sake, or them ... **do** not be a judge
as others who did. Resist the temptation to hold; in your own word and self ignorance; the truth god has
given **unto you**. Let those who open their conscience, behold their god in the name of justice and mercy.

A Paradelle for a Fashion Catalogue Selling Clothing and Sex

Since they were both enamored by the same apparel and accessories, it was love at first sight.
Since they were both enamored by the same apparel and accessories, it was love at first sight.
His natural selection of faux military fashion matched perfectly with her mixed up refugee chic.
His natural selection of faux military fashion matched perfectly with her mixed up refugee chic.
Since his fashion refugee selection of military love apparel matched naturally with her faux chic,
... and they were both enamored by the same mixed up accessories; it was perfect at first sight.

As soon as the price tags were removed, they felt a rush of freedom, a renewal of purpose and of self.
As soon as the price tags were removed, they felt a rush of freedom, a renewal of purpose and of self.
For two people who had nothing better to do than to look the way they do, it was a high like no other.
For two people who had nothing better to do than to look the way they do, it was a high like no other.
As soon as they felt a rush for the highway ... they were like two self-removed people who had no better
of a purpose, than of the freedom to do nothing. And was it a price tags' look of renewal ... to do other?

Conquered by the armies of the Corporate Clothing Empire; only to be displaced by reactionary footwear;
Conquered by the armies of the Corporate Clothing Empire; only to be displaced by reactionary footwear;
a lost and lonely girl met a kind young soldier, without a word, they knew they were made for each other.
a lost and lonely girl met a kind young soldier, without a word, they knew they were made for each other.
Conquered by corporate footwear, the reactionary armies of clothing met without a word; they were young,
and made to be lonely ... only for each other. A kind soldier, displaced by a girl they knew ... lost the empire.

A girl met a soldier who ... enamored by corporate renewal; had nothing to do with a word of natural selection.
The first sight of his military footwear and her rush of reactionary apparel was better than to look at each other.
It was like no other fashion empire ... since the clothing made for the same two perfectly matched armies.
Only a ... they both kind of knew they were young for a chic self love. And lost by the way people do without
high purpose accessories ... and conquered by the mixed up price tags of freedom ... they were displaced
as soon as they ... they were removed. It felt lonely to be a faux refugee.

A Paradelle on the Power of Love

There is no greater power in the world than the force that we all feel, when we fully open our hearts to love,
There is no greater power in the world than the force that we all feel, when we fully open our hearts to love,
the transcendent joy of bliss, pulsing through our embrace of life; and infusing our experience of existence.
the transcendent joy of bliss, pulsing through our embrace of life; and infusing our experience of existence.
And we ... when we open our hearts to fully feel the force of all that bliss, there is no greater life experience
than our embrace of the transcendent joy pulsing through existence, infusing our world in the power of love.

Love is our birthright and purpose. Evolution is not academic, it is the journey of the souls search for grace.
Love is our birthright and purpose. Evolution is not academic, it is the journey of the souls search for grace.
What makes us human is not our intellect alone; our willingness to love secures us our most basic humanity.
What makes us human is not our intellect alone; our willingness to love secures us our most basic humanity.
Human evolution is our birthright; the journey is us, it secures our search for our souls most basic humanity.
Our willingness to love is not the grace of intellect and academic purpose. Love is what makes us not alone.

Love is the divine treasure born within each heartbeat, our cosmic inheritance and potential as spiritual beings.
Love is the divine treasure born within each heartbeat, our cosmic inheritance and potential as spiritual beings.
Through love we become as one with the immeasurable wealth of life, the eternal spirit behind all of creation.
Through love we become as one with the immeasurable wealth of life, the eternal spirit behind all of creation.
Born with the immeasurable inheritance of life within each heartbeat; love is the one divine treasure behind all
spiritual wealth. And as through our creation, as potential cosmic beings; we become the spirit of eternal love.

The immeasurable power and joy of existence; pulsing through our hearts, is our most basic human birthright.
There is no greater purpose to embrace, than the creation of love. Love is the bliss behind our eternal journey;
the cosmic and divine force that we treasure for fully infusing us through grace. Our search secures us as one,
as beings of love; with willingness, spirt and potential. In all of life, love is not the souls academic experience;
the intellect alone is not our wealth. When we feel what our spiritual inheritance is ... our humanity born within
the evolution of each heartbeat ... we become open to all life. It makes transcendent our love of the world.

A Paradelle for What We've Become

Essentially, we are wounded animals, with fictitious cultural identities, defined by tragic personal histories.
Essentially, we are wounded animals, with fictitious cultural identities, defined by tragic personal histories.
As a people, our potential is undermined by cruel and needless suffering. The cause? Our ignorance and fear.
As a people, our potential is undermined by cruel and needless suffering. The cause? Our ignorance and fear.
As animals, we are essentially undermined by suffering with fictitious identities, cultural histories defined by
cruel and tragic people; a wounded potential and our personal fear ... the cause is our needless ignorance.

Sadly, the majority of our time alone with ourselves; we spend ignoring, denying and resisting ... the animal us.
Sadly, the majority of our time alone with ourselves; we spend ignoring, denying and resisting ... the animal us.
The rest of the time society does it for us, reflecting and reinforcing, the marketable and conceptual social self.
The rest of the time society does it for us, reflecting and reinforcing, the marketable and conceptual social self.
And reinforcing the self denying society of the marketable majority; and ignoring our time of rest and reflecting
with our animal selves ... the social time we spend alone ... the conceptual us sadly does the resisting it for us.

Hopefully, we can selfishly begin to heal the broken heart of the beast through the embrace of our human spirit,
Hopefully, we can selfishly begin to heal the broken heart of the beast through the embrace of our human spirit.
Because if your animal isn't getting the love and understanding it needs, it won't be happy and neither will you.
Because if your animal isn't getting the love and understanding it needs, it won't be happy and neither will you.
And if neither of you ... can selfishly begin to heal the animal of your love and willfully embrace the human heart;
won't it be because we; the happy broken beast, isn't getting the hope our spirit needs, through understanding it?

We are essentially suffering animals, selfishly reinforcing our fear through fictitious and tragic social histories.
Our potential as a people is cruelly undermined by our sad and marketable ignorance. And if society defined;
does your denying, and neither of you embrace the wounded self ... won't we alone be resisting the human it?
Will the cultural majority ... and our broken identities ... begin the needless cause of ignoring the spirit for us?
Because the animal isn't conceptual, it needs us to rest and spend time, personal time; reflecting with ourselves.
Hopefully, by understanding the love of the beast, and getting happy with it, we can heal the heart of the animal.

A Paradelle for Personal Transformation

One day, while lifting his leg to a tree; Jack realized that there was more to life than simply dying like a dog.
One day, while lifting his leg to a tree; Jack realized that there was more to life than simply dying like a dog.
Perhaps it was something in the air, a divine scent in the breeze that turned his attention to what he could be.
Perhaps it was something in the air, a divine scent in the breeze that turned his attention to what he could be.
One day, while lifting jack in the air, he realized that a tree could be divine; that there was something more to
the breeze than simply a dying scent. His attention turned to it; to what was perhaps ... like a dogleg in his life.

Poised silently in the pale blue beyond, the moon heard the howl rise up from his soul ... crying out for a witness.
Poised silently in the pale blue beyond, the moon heard the howl rise up from his soul ... crying out for a witness;
deeper than the shallow self he had been. His heartbeat held the connection, to a presence greater than life itself.
Deeper than the shallow self he had been, his heartbeat held the connection, to a presence greater than life itself.
Deeper than the pale blue connection crying out for the moon ... greater than the presence poised to witness itself;
the self beyond a beat he silently held in his heart ... heard a soul rise up from the howl ... his shallow life had been.

The essence of the earth called him back to an awareness ... the sensation of his feet and the ground beneath them.
The essence of the earth called him back to an awareness ... the sensation of his feet and the ground beneath them.
Within his chest breathed a sacred relationship to life; reflected in his eyes ... ever so clearer, and brighter than before.
Within his chest breathed a sacred relationship to life; reflected in his eyes ... ever so clearer, and brighter than before.
An awareness of the ever sacred earth breathed within his feet. The ground beneath them called him back to a clearer
relationship to his eyes ... and the sensation in his chest ... and so brighter, than before .... the reflected essence of life.

One day, in the presence of a greater self ... Jack realized that a heartbeat could be divine, that, beyond the breeze,
there was a pale scent poised in the air, crying out for his attention. In his chest, a shallow sensation called him back
to the howl ... dying ... more to itself than ... to what he had been ... than ... than the witness of his relationship to life.
While his eyes reflected the silent life ... and the moon turned a brighter blue ... he breathed into his feet, and heard
something like a leg rise up from them. Perhaps ... it was the earthly connection to the deeper dog within his soul ...
lifting an awareness beneath the sacred tree. The ground held, so simply, his life essence; clearer than ever before.

A Paradelle for ... If the Buddha's Teaching had Befriended a Dog

If the Buddha, in his enlightenment had befriended a dog, would they have walked together in meditation?
If the Buddha, in his enlightenment had befriended a dog, would they have walked together in meditation?
Alive and awake to the present moment, breathing with each step, both inhaling, exhaling ... no self, no other.
Alive and awake to the present moment, breathing with each step, both inhaling, exhaling ... no self, no other.
If a dog had befriended Buddha with his enlightenment ... would they have walked ... breathing in each step,
exhaling meditation and inhaling the alive moment together ... both awake to the no self present in no other?

With a spirit filled compassion for the suffering of all others, and with an excited, sloppy kiss for condolences;
With a spirit filled compassion for the suffering of all others, and with an excited, sloppy kiss for condolences;
the unambiguous embrace of a dogs heart gives unconditioned comfort to anyone who is in need of love.
the unambiguous embrace of a dogs heart gives unconditioned comfort to anyone who is in need of love.
For anyone who is suffering with a spirit filled with condolences, and for anothers excited, unambiguous kiss.
... the unconditioned comfort of a dog's heart gives the embrace of love to all in need of sloppy compassion.

Seated in concentrated meditation, forever faithful to the eternal now, his attention, is at last free to be pure love,
Seated in concentrated meditation, forever faithful to the eternal now, his attention, is at last free to be pure love,
the dog, upon hearing the call of devotion, rising to its feet, lifted up its ears; the moment Buddha began his walk.
the dog, upon hearing the call of devotion, rising to its feet, lifted up its ears; the moment Buddha began his walk.
Ears hearing the call to be seated in concentrated devotion; Buddha began the *Love is Forever Faithful* meditation.
Free upon its rising up to walk ... at the moment of his eternal now ... his pure attention lifted the last dog to its feet.

Hearing the call to walk for the seated suffering of all others, the Buddha gives his concentrated love to each step.
Breathing condolences into a moment in need of forever, his feet befriended a dog who walked with pure attention.
Rising up together ... and upon inhaling no other moment ... they began exhaling the meditation of unconditioned
compassion. Awake in the unambiguous love of the Buddha, a dogs heart is free to be present with anyone alive.
If it's faithful devotion had no comfort for the dog ... and to have both its ears lifted in the spirit filled now is eternal,
would his sloppy self enlightenment embrace meditation ... with an excited kiss ... at last?

bonus paradelles

from the future series:

a paradelle book of ministries

poetry for the post apocalypse

the paradelles in their order of appearance

a paradelle for a soliloquy: what a funny place I am

what a funny place I am ... here I mean, where lived I be; the curious correspondence of location and common appearance,
what a funny place I am ... here I mean, where lived I be; the curious correspondence of location and common appearance,
born into a world of historical organization and consequences, unceremoniously subtracted from an existence beyond time.
born into a world of historical organization and consequences, unceremoniously subtracted from an existence beyond time.
and what a curious historical appearance I am ... born into an unceremoniously mean world of commonplace consequences,
where ... subtracted from correspondence beyond the here I be; lived a funny I organization of existence, location, and time.

how odd indeed it is to be; this ego identity complex, this self constructed edifice created to eradicate the effects of our nature:
how odd it is indeed to be; this ego identity complex, this self constructed edifice created to eradicate the effects of our nature:
the inherent expression of our vulnerability to the natural world of energies, qualities and divinity; that is native within each of us.
the inherent expression of our vulnerability to the natural world of energies, qualities and divinity; that is native within each of us.
our vulnerability to it, and to this self constructed world of ego expression; created the complex effects of identity. our nature is
to be the natural qualities that eradicate this edifice of odd energies. how native indeed is the inherent divinity within each of us.

were it not for the unusual circumstances surrounding each breath, who here among us now, could authenticate its observation?
were it not for the unusual circumstances surrounding each breath, who here among us now, could authenticate its observation?
not the numerical and most identifiable social self, thinly disguised behind a facade. in order to be seen, the spirit wears a mask.
not the numerical and most identifiable social self, thinly disguised behind a facade. in order to be seen, the spirit wears a mask.
now in order not to be a disguised spirit behind its identifiable circumstances; and were it not for the; the unusual self observation
surrounding each numerical breath ... could the most thinly seen social facade here among us authenticate who wears a mask?

what a funny mask of ego effects I am; a self identity constructed to order for historical observation. unceremoniously numerical,
and odd beyond the consequences of location. in the natural correspondence of time; its expression is subtracted from the world
of appearance ... a facade with an edifice complex. and behind it ... where this organization wears thin ... each place eradicated
who I mean. and were it not our unusual divinity to be us; to be born here among the common circumstances of our most curious
nature; how could the socially created self, surrounding each identifiable breath, authenticate a native vulnerability to the energies
of existence? this inherent spirit world ... and the I qualities now seen in us ... that is indeed, not here ... to be lived in disguise.

a paradelle for being ... impartial to the naked eye

as twilight inches towards sunrise, at the instant of existence, each moment becomes the, ...the entire universe of time and space.
as twilight inches towards sunrise, at the instant of existence, each moment becomes the ... the entire universe of time and space.
vanishing entirely, only to reappear, slightly different with the one vague distinction ... the impression of having been here all along.
vanishing entirely, only to reappear, slightly different with the one vague distinction ... the impression of having been here all along.
as each impression of all existence becomes the ... the entire distinction ... having been one with the only different instant of space
time to reappear here at sunrise; the universe ... inches along towards the entirely vague and slightly vanishing moment of twilight.

somewhere near the boundary of midnight, as a worn face turns back to gaze at darkness, a new day prepares itself to be born.
somewhere near the boundary of midnight, as a worn face turns back to gaze at darkness, a new day prepares itself to be born.
crossing the precarious passage between shadow and light, the grateful breath of the world reverberates, announcing its arrival.
crossing the precarious passage between shadow and light, the grateful breath of the world reverberates, announcing its arrival.
born to be precarious, to gaze at the grateful face announcing midnight ... a new day reverberates somewhere between the worn
boundary of breath and the passage of its arrival. crossing back as the world turns light ... darkness prepares itself near a shadow.

deep in dreamless sleep, our maternal ocean reaches out from within her constant self, restlessly casting waves upon the shore.
deep in dreamless sleep, our maternal ocean reaches out from within her constant self, restlessly casting waves upon the shore.
caressing a crescent moon, starlight surrenders to the embrace of the sky ... at the edge of sight, clouds drift across the horizon.
caressing a crescent moon, starlight surrenders to the embrace of the sky ... at the edge of sight, clouds drift across the horizon.
constant within sight of the sky, the moon reaches out across our maternal horizon. casting her dreamless embrace deeply upon
the shore ... crescent waves drift in from sleep. caressing clouds at the edge of starlight ... a restless self surrenders to the ocean.

crossing at the boundary between her vanishing existence, and the distinction of having a new face; the entire ocean reverberates
with the passage of the moon. worn and indifferent waves drift along the shore; slightly caressing a vague impression of darkness.
as midnight becomes shadow, the edge of space prepares itself to gaze back across the universe; constantly casting each moment
of time. crescent clouds embrace the restless sky. the dreamless arrival of the day reaches out somewhere near the deep horizon.
announcing its been entirely grateful to be here ... all the world ... upon sight of one self born breath ... turns maternal from within.
... at ... at the instant starlight surrenders to our sleep ... a precarious light inches towards sunrise ... only to reappear as twilight.

a paradelle for being a dare devil

Walter was a daredevil, and caution was an evil word; his safety net was the irresponsibility of a system that rewarded recklessness.
Walter was a daredevil, and caution was an evil word; his safety net was the irresponsibility of a system that rewarded recklessness.
even his revival, that could only be the bets, borrowed on a promise and a risk ... could be redeemed by our faith in the god we trust.
even his revival, that could only be the bets, borrowed on a promise and a risk ... could be redeemed by our faith in the god we trust.
Walter was the devil of a net faith, and an evil dare was his only promise. his revival in the recklessness we trust, rewarded the risks
that redeemed our irresponsibility. and could *caution even be a word*? could a safety system be; that was borrowed by god on a bet?

but he was feckless with the future, and gambled with the fortunes of empires and kings; nothing beat the thrill of tempting fate;
but he was feckless with the future, and gambled with the fortunes of empires and kings; nothing beat the thrill of tempting fate;
like falling into a pit filled with snakes, or jumping onto a runaway train. to escape unscathed would require more than a miracle.
like falling into a pit filled with snakes, or jumping onto a runaway train. to escape unscathed would require more than a miracle.
the train was a thrill to escape on ... but jumping into a future fate filled with nothing would require more than tempting a miracle.
and like other pit kings unscathed with beat and falling fortunes, he too gambled with the runaway empires of f-feckless snakes.

daily taunting death by net loss, he flagrantly cut his margins too thin. the ride of one's life is to race along the edge of the abyss.
daily taunting death by net loss, he flagrantly cut his margins too thin. the ride of one's life is to race along the edge of the abyss.
but its dangerous, when the bad luck of the bystanders can influence the momentum of gravity; especially a financial cliffhanger.
but its dangerous, when the bad luck of the bystanders can influence the momentum of gravity; especially a financial cliffhanger.
but he too is taunting the margins of the bad financial ride. especially when a dangerous death race to the thin edge of luck can
influence the gravity of one's life by its momentum. the net loss of his daily cliffhanger flagrantly cut along the bystanders abyss.

Walter gambled with the devil on a dare. he cut along the thin edge of a cliffhanger, tempting gravity with the net loss of his luck.
falling into an evil race we can trust, the kings of irresponsibility and bad risks bet on the influence of momentum and borrowed
fortunes. and even the snakes of a dangerous faith ... unscathed but by the word of god ... could be redeemed to beat its margins.
but by taunting the bystanders with a flagrantly feckless promise; the runaway death that was his daily ride was more like a miracle
jumping to safety than a fate he too could escape. especially, when the future recklessness of a net to nothing empire was his only
pit filled thrill; and the abyss our financial system trains in, is one. or would a caution that was rewarded be the revival life requires?

a paradelle on our need for Jesus

even if Jesus Christ had never existed, never really lived; our need for him is so great that we would have had to invent him.
even if Jesus Christ had never existed, never really lived; our need for him is so great that we would have had to invent him.
but not the scriptural Jesus of salvation and miracles, thats the Jesus who was; we need a Jesus who is living among us now.
but not the scriptural Jesus of salvation and miracles, thats the Jesus who was; we need a Jesus who is living among us now.
our need of great salvation was so us ... that Jesus would have had to had lived among miracles. but a scriptural Christ never
really existed for the living Jesus; thats the Jesus who we need now. and even if we invent him; Jesus is Him who never is not.

and where we need him, is in our hearts and in our experience of each other; the compassion and forgiveness of Christ is divine.
and where we need him, is in our hearts and in our experience of each other; the compassion and forgiveness of Christ is divine.
but is it not in the human heart, the heart that Christ made sacred and offers as a path; that love has the power to heal our pain?
but is it not in the human heart, the heart that Christ made sacred and offers as a path; that love has the power to heal our pain?
and, as in the divine path where Christ is not our pain, and compassion offers it heart, we need the love that Christ made sacred.
but the heart that a human has the power to heal is; is in our hearts experience of Him and; and in our forgiveness of each other.

and in that spirit, we need a Jesus who loves us without judgement; so that we might likewise love our unholy, but worthy selves.
and in that spirit, we need a Jesus who loves us without judgement; so that we might likewise love our unholy, but worthy selves.
even if Jesus never walked a dusty road alone, searching for a friend; our need for his presence in our lives drives us to find him.
even if Jesus never walked a dusty road alone, searching for a friend; our need for his presence in our lives drives us to find him.
but even if we walked alone without searching our holy spirit for a Jesus who loves us; our need for judgement and a dusty road
drives us to need him; a friend that likewise lives in love, so that we; our never unworthy selves, might find Jesus in his presence,

and even if Jesus never really was our salvation, we need him now as a path to our human heart; that we might find forgiveness
among our selves. likewise we need a Jesus Christ that is living where we need him; a Jesus Christ who never walked our road
of unholy pain, that existed but never lived with our judgement; the Jesus who is out searching our worthy hearts for the miracles
his compassion offers in a friend. and, and even if we had the scriptural power to invent him, that alone is not divine. For is it not
in the presence of Jesus Christ; experience has made our love for each other sacred? but, but thats so; so the spirit would have
had us in need of a great love ... and loves need drives him to heal us. and in that heart, is the Jesus ... who lives in dusty us.

a paradelle on the ... influence ... of ... perspectives

marijuana is multi-dimensional, it opens up new horizons and perspectives; the panoramic awareness of an active consciousness.
marijuana is multi-dimensional, it opens up new horizons and perspectives; the panoramic awareness of an active consciousness.
alcohol has a rather narrow line of sight, and a very predictable and linear curve to its stupefying affects on the human animal.
alcohol has a rather narrow line of sight, and a very predictable and linear curve to its stupefying affects on the human animal.
marijuana has an active awareness of the curve to its consciousness; and it opens a new dimensional and multi-panoramic sight
on human horizons. alcohol affects a rather predictable animal ... and the very linear line up of narrow perspectives is stupefying.

some people are more comfortable with a narrow point of view ... and easily irritated by any chance expansion of a singular idea.
some people are more comfortable with a narrow point of view ... and easily irritated by any chance expansion of a singular idea.
for them, marijuana is an attack on their socialized identity and the source of disturbing doubts within their troubled sense of self.
for them, marijuana is an attack on their socialized identity and the source of disturbing doubts within their troubled sense of self.
a sense of their socialized self is disturbing for some people on marijuana. and within them ... comfortable points of view are easily
irritated with a chance doubt ... more troubled by an idea ... and attack any expansion of the singular source of their narrow identity,

cannabis can initiate an expanded state of consciousness; a healing occurs in moments, returning a stressed out soul to its senses.
cannabis can initiate an expanded state of consciousness; a healing occurs in moments, returning a stressed out soul to its senses.
the miseries of pain and illness surrender to its influence, such is the restorative power of spirit, integrating mind and body as one.
the miseries of pain and illness surrender to its influence, such is the restorative power of spirit, integrating mind and body as one.
healing occurs in a restorative state of cannabis consciousness; its power to initiate moments of expanded soul can influence pain
to surrender its miseries; and as such, the body of an illness. one senses the spirit is returning and integrating a stressed out mind.

marijuana is a multi-dimensional restorative for the animal body and its miseries. The more troubled affects of alcohol are an illness.
the disturbing influence of a socialized identity on human consciousness ... is a very narrow mind with rather stupefying view points.
and anyone ... in such a singular state of narrow and linear ideas ... is easily attacked by doubts and a panoramic curve of sight ...
their irritated perspective has them returning to stress out, and line up its predictable sources of pain. and cannabis consciousness,
as it occurs ... can initiate chance moments of soul surrender ... and integrating a comfortable expansion to their sense awareness
of the horizon. an active healing on marijuana opens some people; within the power of its spirit, to an expanded, new sense of self.

a paradelle for .... here I am again

here I am again, walking in the cool blue grey of the evening, the green of the hillside absorbed by a brown tinted shadow.
here I am again, walking in the cool blue grey of the evening, the green of the hillside absorbed by a brown tinted shadow.
pausing to notice, and suspending the usual philosophical self dialogue, my awareness is captured by the colorless trees.
pausing to notice, and suspending the usual philosophical self dialogue, my awareness is captured by the colorless trees.
here, walking in the grey shadow of a tinted self dialogue, brown pausing to notice blue suspending the green, I am again absorbed by the hillside and the trees. my usual philosophical awareness is captured by the colorless cool of the evening.

in this moment, I find myself physically moving through space; trackless in the midst of time, yet witnessed by an eternal Self.
in this moment, I find myself physically moving through space; trackless in the midst of time, yet witnessed by an eternal Self.
looking down at the dusty road before me, passing by beneath my feet with each and every step of the way, it is here that I am.
looking down at the dusty road before me, passing by beneath my feet with each and every step of the way, it is here that I am.
looking within an eternal space, and moving this trackless Self down the throughway ... I find my feet witnessed by every dusty step of the road beneath me. yet it is here, that I am physically by myself in the midst of passing ... at each moment before time.

standing beneath the sky, a night time breeze, scented by its journey, drifts across my face; caressing the circularness of breath.
standing beneath the sky, a night time breeze, scented by its journey, drifts across my face; caressing the circularness of breath.
here, the horizon turns itself towards twilight, and I am again along for the ride; counting the stars between darkness and dawn.
here, the horizon turns itself towards twilight, and I am again along for the ride; counting the stars between darkness and dawn.
standing; for the ride across the nighttime sky; a breeze drifts along between twilight and darkness. scented by the circularness of its journey beneath the stars, my breath turns again towards counting itself. and I am here, face caressing the dawn horizon.

here I am again, pausing in this moment of darkness ... absorbed by the circularness of a dialogue between my usual colorless self and a philosophical shadow. standing along the dusty road before me; trackless across the face of time; physically counting each and every breath of the journey ... the green scented ride turns itself in the sky ... and I am yet again; witnessed by twilight caressing an eternal space. looking at it here ... in the midst of the brown hillside; the self suspending evening breeze is moving down through the trees ... the night time cool drifts by beneath my step ... walking my feet towards the horizon. for I find myself captured by awareness ... I notice am here and ... that the way to grey dawn is tinted with blue by its passing beneath the stars.

a paradelle for being: identified with the pain body ... rather than being the living identity of our bliss body

the failure of our culture is that, rather than being the living identity of our bliss; we are taught to be identified with a body of pain.
the failure of our culture is that, rather than being the living identity of our bliss; we are taught to be identified with a body of pain.
our sense of self is the story of the wounding we've experienced directly from other people in pain, or inherited from our families.
our sense of self is the story of the wounding we've experienced directly from other people in pain, or inherited from our families.
we are taught to be identified with the living pain of our culture, our sense of pain is inherited from the wounding of other people.
or, rather than being the self of body bliss, our identity is in the failure of a story that we've experienced directly from our families.

the tragedy and loss of this is shared by each of us; our humanity suffers constantly and without measure from this ancient error.
the tragedy and loss of this is shared by each of us; our humanity suffers constantly and without measure from this ancient error.
the belief, that in making punishment the counter weight to our ignorance, we can avoid the burden of intelligent self awareness.
the belief, that in making punishment the counter weight to our ignorance, we can avoid the burden of intelligent self awareness.
the belief that we can avoid our awareness of this error; without punishment and loss, suffers from the ancient ignorance shared
by each of us. and the tragedy to humanity is in making this constantly counter intelligent burden the weight of our self measure.

we can return to our natural birthright of bliss, the fundamental state of life on earth, through the embrace of our self compassion;
we can return to our natural birthright of bliss, the fundamental state of life on earth, through the embrace of our self compassion;
the greatest love we can give to the world is the being and beauty of our true selves; the natural joy and generosity of our hearts.
the greatest love we can give to the world is the being and beauty of our true selves; the natural joy and generosity of our hearts.
through the world of joy, the birthright of our beauty; the bliss of being is our true and natural self on earth. can we give ourselves
the greatest love we can, and embrace our return to the fundamental generosity of life; to the hearts natural state of compassion?

we are constantly taught to be self identified with the fundamental failure that we've inherited from our families shared body of pain.
the intelligent return of our natural identity, to a culture of self awareness and compassion, is the greatest measure of love our hearts
can embrace. the counter error we give to the world; is this ancient and living punishment of life on earth. our sense of bliss suffers
from the burden of our ignorance; experienced directly through the weight of other people in pain. or, rather than making the story
to the loss of our true selves ... the tragedy of our belief ... we can ... we can avoid this wounding from without ... by being the joy
and natural beauty that is our self bliss. the state of our generosity is the birthright of our being, and the humanity in each of us.

a paradelle on the deconstruction of an agreement

its funny how people who don't remember any agreements they made with me, won't let me forget one that I've made with them.
its funny how people who don't remember any agreements they made with me, won't let me forget one that I've made with them.
equally so, is the curiosity, of how easily memories become so self convincingly self specific, as to claim sole witness to the truth.
equally so, is the curiosity, of how easily memories become so self convincingly self specific, as to claim sole witness to the truth.
its funny how easily that is ... people with convincingly made me memories; who so don't remember self truth, won't let any specific curiosity become of equal self witness to the one claim I've made with them. how they ... so solely as to me, forget the agreements.

it would seem; that my hallucination of a conversation between us, would be less likely than a convenient denial of its' occurrence.
it would seem; that my hallucination of a conversation between us, would be less likely than a convenient denial of its' occurrence.
the doubles match between: yes you did ... no I didn't; and you did too; I did not, is one of the worst verbal racket games on earth.
the doubles match between: yes you did ... no I didn't: and you did too; I did not, is one of the worst verbal racket games on earth.
would I did too not be a ... a convenient doubles conversation? would it seem likely on earth, that my hallucination of you is no less than one of the worst verbal occurrences of denial between us? did the game between you didn't, and yes I did ... match its racket?

vows of faith not withstanding, the temptation to fabricate reality out performs the safeguards put in place to prevent its alteration.
vows of faith not withstanding, the temptation to fabricate reality out performs the safeguards put in place to prevent its alteration.
it sometimes seems, that it is only by a very thin margin of coincidence, that two people can establish a correspondence of intent.
it sometimes seems, that it is only by a very thin margin of coincidence, that two people can establish a correspondence of intent.
by a safe margin of two people, not only can correspondence establish vows that prevent the alterations of coincidence; it seems sometimes that it is standing guard to outperform the very intent of a thin faith; put in place with temptations, to fabricate its reality.

any agreements made between two people, who don't match equally with a correspondence of reality; fabricate verbal safeguards by the convenient margin of a conversation made with denial. the specific doubles of, yes, no, you did, did not,; is one of the worst games of faith people so convincingly claim witness to. and that occurrence ... as it seems to me, would be its sole racket on earth. vows to self prevent the very temptation it is ... the only intent of coincidence they can establish, that sometimes outperforms them, is a less than likely hallucination that its not self truth. its funny how easily I forget I have my curiosity with me. it would seem I didn't remember ... how to put the one alteration standing between us ... in a place that won't let memories of you did too become so thin.

a paradelle for ... a mind is a terrible thing to misappropriate

the neural and bio-chemical pathways by which we experience the phenomena called mind ... are by no means the mind itself.
the neural and bio-chemical pathways by which we experience the phenomena called mind ... are by no means the mind itself.
our thoughts, are not how we think about ourselves and the world ... rather a reflection; of how our conditioning thinks about us.
our thoughts, are not how we think about ourselves and the world ... rather a reflection; of how our conditioning thinks about us.
our thoughts are not how we mind the world ... and the bio-conditioning phenomena of the mind; are by no means the chemical
experience itself ... rather, how our neural pathways think about a reflection called ourselves; and by which, we thinks about us.

the obvious point of collision; regardless from which direction one arrives at the question ... is trusting too much in our certainties.
the obvious point of collision; regardless from which direction one arrives at the question ... is trusting too much in our certainties.
which brings to mind, a primary assumption; that our essential sense of self is more than an accidental apprehension of the flesh.
which brings to mind, a primary assumption; that our essential sense of self is more than an accidental apprehension of the flesh.
an apprehension of our primary question, is much more essential than the collision of flesh which brings the point to mind. which;
one arrives at from trusting a directionless assumption; that, in regard too our certainties ... the accidental sense of self is obvious.

the potential for damage is purely unguarded; and open ended when placed in a coincidental position of compromise and debate.
the potential for damage is purely unguarded; and open ended when placed in a coincidental position of compromise and debate.
in the slow return to consciousness, the power of our attention is critical in recovering and conserving the character of our minds.
in the slow return to consciousness, the power of our attention is critical in recovering and conserving the character of our minds.
and when the power, for recovering the minds' potential is slow in return; and purely in the position of unguarded compromise and
coincidental damage ... our attention is placed into a debate critical of conserving the open ended character of our consciousness.

the biochemical character coincidental to our mind, thinks about our unguarded neural pathways and the potential for a collision
of positions, an accidental compromise by which we experience ourselves trusting purely in ... the assumptions of a conditioning
called us. we think not about the more obvious reflection, which is how our primary and essential sense of apprehension is itself
critical of the certainties of mind that brings our flesh to consciousness. and which by no means; when too much damage placed
the power of a mind, rather than the phenomena of the mind; in question; how the debate ended. at the point one is directionless,
and self regard is recovering in the open return, our thoughts are ... are slow and arrive in the world from conserving our attention.

a paradelle for a so-called health care no. two

since my doctor wasn't able to remove the symptoms of my illness, he assumed that there was something wrong with my mind.
since my doctor wasn't able to remove the symptoms of my illness, he assumed that there was something wrong with my mind.
so I was sent to see the shrink upstairs, who; from her examination, could determine, whether I needed drugs or psychotherapy.
so I was sent to see the shrink upstairs, who; from her examination, could determine, whether I needed drugs or psychotherapy.
the examination wasn't able to determine whether her mind could shrink from my symptoms. so, to remove who I see; my doctor
sent drugs that needed psychotherapy. or he assumed, since there was the I of illness ... something with my upstairs was wrong.

I decide to see a specialist ... thinking; if something escaped the gaze of a generalist; it might be more obvious to a practiced eye.
I decide to see a specialist ... thinking; if something escaped the gaze of a generalist; it might be more obvious to a practiced eye.
but instead of looking at the sentence structure of my condition, for tone or grammatical errors; he can't see past the punctuation.
but instead of looking at the sentence structure of my condition, for tone or grammatical errors; he can't see past the punctuation
to see the condition of it. but instead of thinking he ... a past specialist at sentence punctuation ... can't see if something escaped
a structure of errors or my eye; I decide the practiced gaze might be more obvious to a grammatical generalist looking for the tone.

since the symptom is the cause of the complaint, elimination of the symptom is a return to wellness; which is being symptom free.
since the symptom is the cause of the complaint, elimination of the symptom is a return to wellness; which is being symptom free.
and as a statement of fact: the paragraphs of disclaimers of dangerous side effects, one must read before starting the treatment.
and as a statement of fact: the paragraphs of disclaimers of dangerous side effects, one must read before starting the treatment.
one dangerous symptom of the disclaimer is the elimination of wellness ... the cause being the symptoms return to the complaint.
which is as before, and is since starting the paragraph of must read symptoms, a side effect of a statement of fact free treatments.

since my complaint wasn't able to remove the symptom ... it was obvious that the cause of my condition escaped the elimination
of grammatical errors. so my doctor, who could determine the side effects of her examination; was sent upstairs to see if looking
at a specialist assumed the symptoms of the disclaimer. but since he is more of a generalist, he can't see the sentence structure;
which is starting to shrink past the punctuation. thinking there might be something wrong with psychotherapy, I needed to decide;
being something eye and I must see ... whether I return the symptoms of dangerous drugs ... as a one fact statement of wellness;
or instead ... my illness before treatment. for the gaze of a practiced mind, is free to read paragraphs from the tone of a symptom.

a paradelle for the fang mouthed fascists barking for the radical far right

in the hierarchy of heroes stand the defenders of a great moral wasteland; shriekers and criers of dire warnings and alarm.
in the hierarchy of heroes stand the defenders of a great moral wasteland; shriekers and criers of dire warnings and alarm.
embracing the commonplace opinions of the unthinking and misinformed ... their lies and half truths slip by as wise advice.
embracing the commonplace opinions of the unthinking and misinformed ... their lies and half truths slip by as wise advice.
in the great moral hierarchy of misinformed shriekers; stand the unthinking defenders of half heroes and commonplace lies.
... and as the warnings and opinions of criers embracing a wasteland ... truths dire and wise slip by the advice of their alarm.

sucking blood from the unborn by a tax on their soul ... pillaging their future heartbreak beneath the burdens of the betrayed;
sucking blood from the unborn by a tax on their soul ... pillaging their future heartbreak beneath the burdens of the betrayed;
who ... has given themselves the right; while denying rites to the dead, to prey upon the sovereign life potential of the living?
who ... has given themselves the right; while denying rites to the dead, to prey upon the sovereign life potential of the living?
sucking the sovereign right of life from their prey; pillaging on the burdens beneath the blood tax upon the unborn ... who? ...
while dead to themselves; has betrayed the living potential of the future, by denying their soul the rites given to a heartbreak?

protecting the minds of the ignorant, from all threats posed by progressive thought, the security of obedience silences dissent.
protecting the minds of the ignorant, from all threats posed by progressive thought, the security of obedience silences dissent.
the language of intolerance needs no translation in the eyes of the innocent ... words disappear in a blind totality of repression.
the language of intolerance needs no translation in the eyes of the innocent ... words disappear in a blind totality of repression.
from the totality of a minds blind obedience; intolerance silences the innocent language of progressive dissent. in the translation
of threats posed by the security of repression ... all the needs of *NO!!!!!* disappear in the thought words protecting ignorant eyes.

as the criers of moral lies prey upon the betrayed; denying the totality of threats posed by themselves ... the heartbreak heroes
of progressive silence stand in a half living wasteland of ignorant shriekers ... embracing a dire hierarchy of misinformed alarm.
and in protecting the unborn blood of the future ... from the dead to rights defenders of the repression of all sovereign language
and truths ... the innocent, who dissent by pillaging unthinking opinions from potential obedience; disappear beneath the words
and burdens of the security tax on intolerance. and while the rite has given their mind to a great souls commonplace translation;
... in the warnings of their wise advice ... the no their life needs ... slips by ... the thought sucking eyes of the living blind.

a paradelle for life on planet earth

we are manifestations of self awareness in a biological world, where conflict and dispute is resolved through violence and threat.
we are manifestations of self awareness in a biological world, where conflict and dispute is resolved through violence and threat.
a paradise boundaried by punishment and pain, a suffering hell maintained by the guardians of self centered ignorance and fear.
a paradise boundaried by punishment and pain, a suffering hell maintained by the guardians of self centered ignorance and fear.
we are manifestations in a hell centered world, where suffering the ignorance of paradise is maintained by threat and punishment.
a self dispute boundaried by guardians of violence and pain ... conflict and fear, and resolved through a biological self awareness.

our predicament is ancient, and passed down through each generation by a statutory wounding to the raw flesh of our innocence.
our predicament is ancient, and passed down through each generation by a statutory wounding to the raw flesh of our innocence.
this inherited curse upon our animal body, bullied and beaten into us as children, creates the confusion and rage locked within us.
this inherited curse upon our animal body, bullied and beaten into us as children, creates the confusion and rage locked within us.
a statutory confusion, and this ancient wounding to our innocence; creates the inherited curse of our flesh. within each generation
is the rage passed down upon us as children. and through our beaten and bullied animal body, locked into us by raw predicament

but beyond the demands of kill or die, a divine awareness enters into our primary planetary experience; kind and constant in love.
but beyond the demands of kill or die; a divine awareness enters into our primary planetary experience; kind and constant in love.
a reliable witness to an emerging consciousness, transcendent in nature, shifting old realities to a new potentiality beyond duality.
a reliable witness to an emerging consciousness, transcendent in nature, shifting old realities to a new potentiality beyond duality.
but beyond our potentiality to enter into a primary nature ... the constant demands of love divines an emerging planetary awareness.
a witness consciousness ... transcendent to old; shifting and beyond reliable realities ... a new kill in kind or die in duality experience.

we are manifestations of innocence, suffering in a fear centered hell. but beyond this predicament; locked within biological realities
and the statutory curse of duality ... a shifting planetary consciousness enters into our primary pain and inherited confusion; where
beyond the threat of punishment ... a kill or die dispute resolved through love is new to nature; and transcendent to our ignorance:
a self conflict boundaried by our ancient rage and maintained by raw violence and ... the constant demands beaten into us by kind
old guardians wounding children in paradise. and as an animal body *is* upon us ... in a world passed down through the bullied flesh
of each generation; a reliable experience and Self awareness; creates a witness to our emerging divine awareness and potentiality.

a paradelle for the making of Dr. Frankenswine's monsters

the morons of materialism, are promoting genetically modified pig hearts as a replacement to worn out and failing human counterparts.
the morons of materialism, are promoting genetically modified pig hearts as a replacement to worn out and failing human counterparts.
the immune response of conscience; rejects the rational excuse for reducing the heart to the function of a biological pump.
the immune response of conscience; rejects the rational excuse for reducing the heart to the function of a biological pump.
and as the immune functions of a biological materialism are modified ... reducing the counter heart for genetically failing to pump,
the human heart response to the rational morons worn out excuse of a conscience rejects the promoting of pig replacement parts.

while recognized as very intelligent and affectionate mammals; and given that some people prefer pigs over dogs as pets;
while recognized as very intelligent and affectionate mammals; and given that some people prefer pigs over dogs as pets;
a pig heart beating beneath a human breast; is nonetheless, alien to the subtleties of emotion; and incapable of human love.
a pig heart beating beneath a human breast; is nonetheless, alien to the subtleties of emotion; and incapable of human love.
and while human and mammal emotions prefer affectionate dogs ... and some intelligent pigs ... over incapable people as pets;
given that the very beating heart of a pig ... is nonetheless recognized beneath subtleties of love ... as alien to a human breast,

self righteous scientific pseudo gods celebrate the ethics of genetic manipulation by harvesting the internal organs of pigs.
self righteous scientific pseudo gods celebrate the ethics of genetic manipulation by harvesting the internal organs of pigs.
myopically ignore the morality of reengineering living animal bodies; as reserve spare parts for diseased and dying people.
myopically ignore the morality of reengineering living animal bodies; as reserve spare parts for diseased and dying people.
as bodies of morality and pseudo living ignore the internal for scientific, by harvesting the genetic reserve of spare pig parts,
self righteous manipulation, myopically celebrates the diseased ethics of gods dying people ... reengineering animal organs.

while recognized as a counter part to the failing ethics of alien manipulation ... scientifically modified pig hearts are nonetheless
affectionate and incapable of ignoring the genetic subtleties of animal emotion. and as the materialism promoting reengineering
the replacement of conscience ... given the god response of the human heart that some people prefer to a pigs rational excuse;
the love function of the human heart is very intelligent and celebrates a biological morality beating beneath a dogs dying breast.
and as for immune morons living as pseudo pig people ... myopically self righteous rejects reduce genetic pigs ... to the bodies
internal reserves of ... of spare pump parts ... by over harvesting human organs for diseased mammals and worn out pets.

a paradelle for the Goddess Maat ... revisited

the Goddess Maat was the ancient Egyptian embodiment and shared experience of: truth; balance, order, morality, law and justice; the Goddess Maat was the ancient Egyptian embodiment and shared experience of: truth; balance, order, morality, law and justice; the constitutional spirit and founding principals of their civilization; for sustaining their society, that held constant within her embrace. the constitutional spirit and founding principals of their civilization; for sustaining their society, that held constant within her embrace. the Goddess sustaining their constant experience of truth ... the founding order and balance for Egyptian civilization that was Maat; held justice and law within her constitutional embodiment. an ancient spirit embraced the shared, morality principals of their society.

from the light of every star in the sky; to the rhythms of life on earth; Maat maintains the cosmic bond, inherent within all that exists. from the light of every star in the sky; to the rhythms of life on earth; Maat maintains the cosmic bond, inherent within all that exists. within her presence, which is woven within the fabric of all that is, chaos remains among the unborn; only to emerge in her absence. within her presence, which is woven within the fabric of all that is, chaos remains among the unborn; only to emerge in her absence. from the cosmic rhythm of her remains in the unborn sky ... only to emerge into the fabric of life, with her all in all presence on earth; the light that exists among the stars, which is woven within every bond that Maat maintains; is inherent within the absence of chaos.

in the peoples hearts; in their daily conduct and relationships with each other ... Maat preserved the power of an honest conscience. in the peoples hearts, in their daily conduct and relationships with each other ... Maat preserved the power of an honest conscience. in the *Hall of Two Truths;* the souls of the dead were weighed within her feathers field of gravity; innocence is freedom from remorse. in the *Hall of Two Truths;* the souls of the dead were weighed within her feathers field of gravity; innocence is freedom from remorse. within the field of her feathers power ... two hearts, in the innocence of an honest relationship and each others conduct ... preserved their souls freedom from gravity. dead truths were weighed daily within the halls of remorse. the conscience of the people is in Maat.

the gravity of ancient Egyptian law remains preserved within the daily relationship of two sustaining principals; each the peoples light on earth: the embodiment of Maat within the conduct of power and the spirit of justice her constant presence maintains within society. cosmic truths that exist in among the stars, were their founding constitutional freedoms, woven within the rhythms of an honest heart. Maat is balance to all life ... every civilization is weighed within her feathers embrace. for unborn conscience to emerge from chaos ... from that which is other and dead in the sky ... the bond within her soul held the inherent fabric that experiences her all and only. in the hall of shared truths; the Goddess Maat was their field of innocence ... in the absence of morality and order ... their remorse.

a paradelle for ... the dog at the door ... version # 2

blessed are we to receive the presence of the dog at our door; and the reassurance of his muffled bark, barely draped in breath.
blessed are we to receive the presence of the dog at our door; and the reassurance of his muffled bark, barely draped in breath.
bathing in the radiant glow of the sun; sleeping in a place of well worn comfort; our alert guardian remains vigilant in his dreams.
bathing in the radiant glow of the sun; sleeping in a place of well worn comfort; our alert guardian remains vigilant in his dreams.
our dog breath blessed guardian; aglow at the door of radiant presence; sleeping in the comfort of well worn dreams; bathing in the barely muffled alert we are to receive, draped in the vigilant remains of his bark, and our reassurance of his place in the sun.

patiently waiting for our return, suffering his loneliness with an unfailing forbearance, watching the emptiness of the day drag along;
patiently waiting for our return, suffering his loneliness with an unfailing forbearance, watching the emptiness of the day drag along;
sphinx like on the floor, all four paws placed in position for standing; actively listening for a certain sound, approaching from far away.
sphinx like on the floor, all four paws placed in position for standing; actively listening for a certain sound, approaching from far away.
his sphinx like forbearance watching the waiting emptiness; with four paws placed in an unfailing standing position, actively suffering for the drag of a certain sound on the floor, for listening all day long ... patiently for our approaching return from a far away loneliness.

a joyous dog at the door; excited to be seen and eager to be inside; our love reaffirmed in a glad and grateful exchange of greetings.
a joyous dog at the door; excited to be seen and eager to be inside; our love reaffirmed in a glad and grateful exchange of greetings.
speaking clearly with a leash gripped between his teeth, testifying to the truth of an immediate need; pleading that it's time for a walk.
speaking clearly with a leash gripped between his teeth, testifying to the truth of an immediate need; pleading that it's time for a walk.
between testifying that it's time to be gripped with a leash and the eager need of a glad truth; speaking inside to a clearly excited dog reaffirmed an immediate exchange of pleading greetings; and grateful for a walk ... the love to be seen in his joyous teeth at our door.

our blessed guardian; testifying to the radiant glow of an immediate presence, speaking joyous greetings with a glad and eager bark, patiently vigilant in his loneliness; watching, a well worn leash, in it's position on the floor, bathing in the remains of the sun, sleeping like a sphinx gripped between his far away dreams and the unfailing reassurance of an alert truth ... standing at our door and draped in the dog breath we are to receive ... suffering ... the emptiness of his barely active teeth, for a need to place a timely comfort within the muffled forbearance of the day, clearly pleading for all four paws to be placed inside of a grateful walk, for being that certain dog, seen listening for our sound approach. in excited exchange at the door ... his love reaffirmed our return from the long drag of waiting.

a paradelle for: embryological nostalgia and its inevitable deja vu ... version one

Epithesis of Demaskus was a worried man, his thoughts favored the skeptical and fictitious imaginings of his insecurities and fears.
Epithesis of Demaskus was a worried man, his thoughts favored the skeptical and fictitious imaginings of his insecurities and fears.
his neighbors couldn't understand him; none but his dog, saw beyond the facade of his fatalism, into the deeper realms of his heart.
his neighbors couldn't understand him; none but his dog, saw beyond the facade of his fatalism, into the deeper realms of his heart.
his thoughts couldn't understand the insecurities of his heart. realms of his facade worried him. a skeptical man, saw into and beyond
the deeper fears and imaginings of his thesis. Epideus, his neighbors; none but ... fictitious dog; was the favored mask of his fatalism.

buried beneath the pain of an unrealized life; the recollection of a memory from his distant past; emerged as a man coming up for air.
buried beneath the pain of an unrealized life; the recollection of a memory from his distant past; emerged as a man coming up for air.
shipwrecked on rocks defined by their curious attraction; each tragic loss exposes the error, of letting ones mind drift out with the tide.
shipwrecked on rocks defined by their curious attraction; each tragic loss exposes the error, of letting ones mind drift out with the tide.
by letting each one of the recollections for life's distant attraction drift on ... their memory of a man without air defined the curious pain
of a shipwrecked past. the error beneath his buried loss emerged, as rocks coming up from the tragic tide expose an unrealized mind

despite the redundancies inherent in a false interpretation of fate; Heliodetritus unveiled the obvious ... and never strayed from home.
despite the redundancies inherent in a false interpretation of fate; Heliodetritus unveiled the obvious ... and never strayed from home.
the infant he; was recognized as a reliable witness to both a moment of truth and the passage of time, he was very well remembered.
the infant he; was recognized as a reliable witness to both a moment of truth and the passage of time, he was very well remembered.
despite the unrecognized passage of a reliable truth; Heliodetritus was both the in-home, inherent, well remembered moment of fate;
and the very obvious witness to false redundancies. and as the a, infant he was; he never strayed from a veiled interpretation of time.

the thesis of Epidetritus shipwrecked his facade. his attraction to the deeper realms of error unveiled a fictitious witness to a tragic life
for buried beneath the redundancies of the tide, was a man defined by the passage of time and in the re-imagining of his insecurities.
his fatalism favored both his well remembered fears, and a past interpretation of pain. a worried dog never strayed from his thoughts.
despite the skeptical loss his distant neighbors saw within their inherent memory of him ... the heart of Heliodeus exposes each mans
infant collection of false airs. and as a curious mind was letting an obvious moment drift home ... none but the mask of fate emerged,
as from the up and coming rocks. he couldn't understand, he was one unrecognized truth ... out on the very reliable, realized beyond.

Author Bio ... Old Man Crowe

Writing lyrical poetry has been the main passion and pursuit in my life for over 45 years; my primary method to understand and make sense of the world as I experienced it.

The last eight years have been devoted to writing Paradelles; a process that has captured my attention and commandeered my time to such a degree that's it has often been my sole and singular focus. I simply love the challenge of the blank page.

My commitment to using the Paradelle form as a vehicle to tell a particular kind of story, to allow the words to tell their own tale ... has been and continues to be ... one of the most rewarding creative efforts that I've ever been engaged in.

This process has been a developmental as well as spiritual gift, one that has benefited my life on more levels than I could name. A gift that will forever be; a foundation and inspiration in my life.

My father wrote poetry and sculpted in clay; and it is from him that I inherited the eye to sculpt in verse and a textural format. My work is not only to communicate to the heart and the mind; but as much as possible ... to speak directly to the visual eye.

In terms of speaking, and the value and importance of the ear; the role of the voice, a Paradelle is also a poetic performance. My next project is to record the audio versions of these poems.